W9-CNC-446

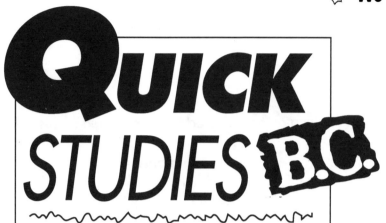

QUICK STUDIES B.C.

Isaiah – Malachi

Cook Ministry Resources
a division of Cook Communications Ministries
Colorado Springs, Colorado/Paris, Ontario

The following authors and editors contributed to this volume:

Stan Campbell
Eric Potter
Randy Southern
Mark Syswerda
Jim Townsend, Ph.D.

Quick Studies B.C.
Isaiah—Malachi: The Books of Prophecy

© 1994 David C. Cook Publishing Co.

Unless otherwise noted, Scripture quotations are from the Holy Bible, New International Version (NIV), © 1973, 1978, 1984 by International Bible Society. Used by permission of Zondervan Bible Publishers.

Published by David C. Cook Publishing Co.
850 North Grove Ave., Elgin, IL 60120
Cable address: DCCOOK
Designed by Bill Paetzold
Cover illustrations by Mick Coulas
Inside illustrations by Michael Fleishman
Printed in U.S.A.

ISBN: 0-7814-5160-4

CONTENTS

ISAIAH

JEREMIAH

LAMENTATIONS

EZEKIEL

DANIEL

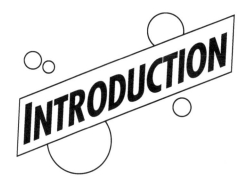

Quick Questions about Quick Studies

We've made *Quick Studies B.C.* as self-explanatory as possible, so you can dive in and start using them right away. But just in case you were wondering . . .

When should I use *Quick Studies B.C.*?
Whenever you want high school or junior high kids to explore the Bible face-to-face and absorb it into their lives. We've kept the openers active and the discussion questions creative, so you can use *Quick Studies B.C.* with confidence in Sunday school, midweek youth Bible study, small groups, even youth group meetings and retreats.

What's so quick about *Quick Studies B.C.*?
They're designed to save you preparation time. The session plans are compact, for quick reading. There aren't a lot of materials to gather, either (you'll need Bibles, pencils and paper, copies of the reproducible sheets, and sometimes a few other items). Yet *Quick Studies B.C.* are *real* Bible studies, with plenty of thought-provoking discussion and life application.

How are these different from other youth Bible studies?
We like to think *Quick Studies B.C.* are . . .
• *Irresistible.* You already know most kids don't jump at the chance to fill in a bunch of blanks in a boring study guide. So we used creative, reproducible sheets and *active* activities to draw kids into Scripture.
• *Involving.* You need discussion *starters*, not discussion *stoppers*. We avoided dull "yes or no" questions and included lots of thought-provokers that should get your group members talking about important issues. And we didn't forget suggested *answers* to most of the tougher questions, which should make things easier for you.
• *Inductive.* Many Bible studies try to force-feed kids a single "aim" and ignore other points Scripture is trying to make. *Quick Studies B.C.* let kids discover a variety of key principles in a passage.
• *Influential.* It's not enough to know what the Bible says. Every session includes a step designed to help kids decide what to do *personally* with vital points from the passage.

When do kids read the passages covered?

That's up to you. If your group is into homework, assign the passages in advance. If not, take time to read the Scripture together after the "Opening Act" step that kicks off each session. There are dozens of ways to read a passage—with volunteers taking turns, or with a narrator and actors "performing" a scene, or with kids underlining points as they read silently, or with you reading as the author and kids listening as the original audience, or with small groups paraphrasing as they read . . .

What if I want to cover more—or less—than a chapter in a session?

Quick Studies B.C. are flexible. Each 45- to 60-minute session covers a chapter of the Old Testament, but you can adjust the speed to fit your group. To cover more than one passage in a session, just pick the points you want to emphasize and drop the activities, questions, and reproducible sheets you don't need. To cover less than a chapter, you may need to add a few questions and spend more time discussing the "So What?" application step in detail.

Do I have to cover a whole Old Testament book?

No. Each session stands alone. Use sessions one at a time if you want to, or mix and match books in any order you choose. No matter how you use them, *Quick Studies B.C.* are likely to help your group see Bible study in a whole new light.

Randy Southern, Series Editor

ISAIAH 1

Get the Message?

OVERVIEW

The prophet Isaiah shares with the people of Israel a message he received from God—and the message is not a pleasant one. God's people have drifted away from Him. They are a sinful and rebellious nation—a truth that God expresses in no uncertain terms. Yet God also makes it clear that there is hope for them if they are willing to become obedient again.

OPENING ACT

Conduct some roleplays in which kids must communicate bad news to others. As they do, see how willing they are to come right out and say what needs to be said. Are they direct, even though the news is bad? Or do they "beat around the bush" so that it's difficult to know what they're trying to communicate? Here are some possible roleplay situations:

• The coach has left it to Martin, his student assistant, to explain to Delray that Delray is getting cut from the team. Martin and Delray are best friends, and Delray's ultimate desire is to make the team.

• Manny and Danita have been dating for a year, but Danita has started liking Ramon. She needs to break up with Manny.

• Jill asked Chris to watch her dog one weekend while she was out of town. But the dog broke its leash and got hit by a car. Chris rushed it to the vet, but it may die. Chris needs to tell Jill what happened. Jill loves her dog very much.

DATE I USED THIS SESSION _____ GROUP I USED IT WITH _____

NOTES FOR NEXT TIME _____

_____

_____

1. Have you ever had to tell someone something that he or she didn't want to hear? If so, what were the circumstances? How did you break the news? How did the person respond? How did you feel?

what Kind of people give bad news to others? work relations?

2. Are you the kind of person who likes to get bad news out in the open so you can deal with it, or would you rather not even know about something bad until you absolutely *have* to do something about it? Give some specific examples.

3. Read Isaiah 1:1-9. **God doesn't have any trouble telling people the truth—even when it's something they'd rather not hear. How do you think Isaiah felt about having to pass the message along to God's people? Explain.** (The messengers of bad news weren't always well received.)

4. **Can you find any good news in Isaiah 1:1-9?** (God still saw the people as His "children" [1:2]. A few "survivors" prevented the country from being totally worthless [1:9].)

5. **According to Isaiah 1:10-17, the people were still offering sacrifices and doing a lot of the things God had told them to do. So what was the problem?** (Though the people were going through the motions of worship, their attitude left a lot to be desired.)

6. **If God finds "no pleasure in the blood of bulls and lambs and goats"** (1:11), **why did He institute animal sacrifice in the first place?** (It was symbolic of the blood that Jesus would eventually shed. But the obedience of the worshiper was always more important than the sacrifice itself.)

7. **God says, "Even if you offer many prayers, I will not listen"** (1:15). **If this is true, then why do we bother to pray when we've done something really bad?** (Sincere prayer and repentance are demonstrated by caring, fair actions [1:16, 17]. Such prayer will be heard by God. But simply mouthing the words of a prayer without backing it up with appropriate behavior does little good. Our worship must be sincere.)

8. Read Isaiah 1:18-31. **Was God giving up on His people? Explain.** (No. God would willingly redeem anyone who repented [1:18, 27]. Yet people who maintained a rebellious attitude would have no hope of redemption.)

9. **Have you ever done something so bad that you felt God must have given up on you? If so, what made you think that?**

10. **When you do things you regret, how sincere is your repentance? Do you ever pray, "Please forgive me" when you don't actually have any real intention of changing your behavior? How can you be more sincere when you pray?**

The reproducible sheet, "The Symbol Truth," portrays a number of images used in Isaiah 1 and then asks group members to create their own images that symbolize their current spiritual status. Some of your group members' images may be positive and others, like most of the biblical ones, may be somewhat negative. After a few minutes, let volunteers show what they've drawn. Close the session with a discussion of how important it is not to neglect one's spiritual life for too long. Emphasize God's willingness to forgive. Point out that the only thing that can limit His power is our own stubborn insistence on doing things our own way rather than His. God can bless His people and give them all they need, but we must be willing to receive His gifts with gratitude.

The Symbol Truth

Isaiah 1 contains many symbols to describe the spiritual condition of God's people. Some of these symbols are pretty strange. A number of them are illustrated below. But, hey, this is the 90s. Surely you can come up with some better images for people to relate to other than "a hut in a field of melons" (1:8). Think of your own current spiritual condition and an appropriate way to symbolize it (whether good or bad—just be honest). Draw your symbol(s) to the best of your ability in the space provided.

Is Your Spiritual Life Like . . .

A body with an injured head, an afflicted heart, and sores from head to foot? (1:5, 6)

A once-faithful woman who has become a hooker? (1:21)

A garden without water? (1:30)

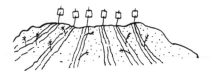

A city under siege? (1:8)

An oak with fading leaves? (1:30)

A mighty man burning up? (1:31)

My Own Spiritual Life Might Be Symbolized as Follows . . .

ISAIAH 5

Say "Whoa" or Say "Woe"

The prophet Isaiah continues his exposition of the vision he received from the Lord. In it, God compares His disobedient people to a vineyard, lovingly planted and cultivated, that yields only bad fruit. His logical question is "Why spend so much time and effort on something that yields nothing good?" He then lists a number of actions for which offenders should expect only "woe" as a result. Such actions include becoming too eager to drink, confusing the clear lines between good and evil, being too self-assured, and more.

(Needed: Blindfold, prizes, penalty items)

Play "Who Do You Trust?" Call for three volunteers at a time. One should be blindfolded. One of the remaining two should have a prize and the other should have some kind of penalty. Both should try to persuade the blindfolded person that he or she is the one with the reward. The blindfolded person must choose and receive what the person has, whether good or bad. Rewards might include candy treats or half dollars. Penalties might involve being shot with a squirt gun.

DATE I USED THIS SESSION _____ GROUP I USED IT WITH _____

NOTES FOR NEXT TIME _____

_____

_____

1. Decribe a time when you went to a lot of trouble to plan something or do a special favor for someone, only to have the person not care or even notice what you'd done. How did you feel? Did you ever want to do anything special for that person again? Why or why not?

2. Can you think of anything God has done for you lately that you haven't noticed or haven't seemed to care about? How do you think God feels when we don't recognize what He's done for us?

3. During the period of time when Isaiah was writing, people were especially blind to the things God had done for them. What imagery did Isaiah use to describe the situation (5:1-7)? (God is portrayed as a caring builder and caretaker of a vineyard that produced only bad fruit.) **Do you see any difference between the description of people then and most of the people you know today? Explain.**

4. Think of your current spiritual condition in terms of a cluster of grapes. Describe yourself in terms of color, texture, sweetness, and so forth.

5. After symbolically expressing His disappointment with the state of the vineyard, God gets more specific about six things He is displeased with. His first "woe" is pronounced on those who are materialistic at the expense of others (5:8). **How does God respond when people try to hoard land or other possessions (5:9, 10)?** (Quantity doesn't guarantee abundance. God determines productivity. With His blessing, a little can produce a lot. Without it, a large amount can produce very little.)

6. The second "woe" was on people who live to party, with little concern for the things of God (5:11, 12). **Do you know people like this? Have you witnessed any of the consequences of Isaiah 5:13-17 in their lives?** (Some group members may know of peers who have died from drug use, drunk driving, or other consequences of a "party" lifestyle, or of those who have been "humbled" in other ways.)

7. The next category is people who seem to carry sin with them wherever they go, as if dragging it along with ropes (5:18, 19). **Do you know of people who seem to expect God to work in their lives, even though they won't give up the wrong things they're doing? Without giving names, what are some examples?**

8. Next are those "who call evil good and good evil" (5:20). **What are some sins that people try to pass off as acceptable practices?** (Drinking; divorce; cheating, as long as "everybody's doing it"; etc.)

9. The fifth "woe" was directed to "those who are wise in their own eyes and clever in their own sight" (5:21). **Do you know people like this? What do you think of such people? Are** *you* **ever guilty of this practice? Explain.**

10. The sixth and final "woe" is for those who "are heroes at drinking wine" and who are dishonest and corrupt as well (5:22, 23). **The people in Isaiah's time were going to be captured by their enemies and taken into captivity (5:24-30). How does a similarly sinful lifestyle take people captive today?** (Alcoholism is a terrible addiction for many people. Similarly, once someone begins a lifestyle based on lies and deceit, it becomes very hard to "go straight" later on.)

11. **Which of the problems described in Isaiah 5 do you think are most threatening to young people today? Why?**

God knew the sins of His people very well. Your kids are likely to be aware of specific sins at their schools and in their neighborhoods. The reproducible sheet, "The Woes Bowl," asks them to record such behavior as well as what they would anticipate the ultimate result of such behavior to be. Kids should be able to come up with quite an assortment of sinful and offensive behavior. Close by affirming that God knows exactly what is going on and will judge accordingly. Rather than being drawn into things that are questionable, we should stand firm and continue to do what we know is right. Only then can we be sure of long-lasting success and satisfaction.

The Woes Bowl

God gave Isaiah a very specific message to give to His people. The message included a number of "woes" and coming judgments. But that was a long time ago. Today's generation has its own behaviors that are just as bad—or worse. And it's not likely that you have to look outside your school or neighborhood to find several examples of such behavior. Suppose it was up to you to bring a warning to the people you know who are not acting the way they should. What would you say to them? We've started a list below. Fill in the blanks with whatever comes to mind, and then add as many other "woes" as you can think of to the end of the list.

Woe to you people at school who pick on weaker people and call them names like

_____ and _____. One day as you stand before God, you

will be the weaker person, and God will call you _____.

Woe to you who cheat your way through school and make grades you don't deserve. Later

in life when you try the same thing, you're going to _____.

Woe to you who ignore me. Though I may choose to forgive you, your behavior is likely to

cause you to _____.

Woe to you who treat teachers as if they were _____. People who

don't respect authority will end up like _____.

Woe to you who seem to think you're so _____. If you don't change the

way you behave, one day you're going to _____.

Finally, Woe to you who _____ because

_____.

ISAIAH 6

Give Me a Call

OVERVIEW

While relating the message God has given him for the people of Israel, Isaiah takes just enough time in his narrative to provide a personal testimony. He describes his vision of God and his call into the ministry. Isaiah's is a calling that is symbolic of everyone who has ever chosen to work for God. He is truthful about his own feelings of inadequacy and explains how God can work through people in spite of their shortcomings—if those people are only willing to serve in the first place.

OPENING ACT

(Needed: Lipstick)

Have kids form teams for a relay. Each team should stand in a single-file line, with the first person in each line facing you. Use a tube of cheap lipstick to create a large smear on the nose of the first person in each line. See which team can be first to pass the lipstick smear all the way to the person in the rear simply by rubbing noses (Person 1 to Person 2, Person 2 to Person 3, and so forth). As soon as the lipstick smear is visible on the face of the last person in line, you can declare a winner. Afterward, point out that proper lip care is important, because Isaiah shows us that our lips may be more significant than we think.

DATE I USED THIS SESSION _____ GROUP I USED IT WITH _____

NOTES FOR NEXT TIME _____

_____

_____

1. People often talk about trying to be "closer to God." But if God suddenly appeared here in the middle of our meeting in all of His glory, what do you think would happen? What, specifically, do you think *you* would do?

2. Isaiah had a vision of God (6:1-3). And in the vision, God was not alone. Even God's attendants would be enough to scare most of us. Where was God's location? (He was manifesting Himself in the temple. Perhaps Isaiah was in the temple when he had his vision, or perhaps the reference is to the heavenly temple.) **When you go to church, do you have any sense of expectation of "seeing" God more clearly? Explain.**

3. Many of Isaiah's senses were at work. What did he see? What did he hear? What did he feel? What do you suppose he smelled?

4. If you had been in Isaiah's place, what might have been your reaction? What might you have thought? What might you have done? Compare group members' responses to Isaiah's reaction in Isaiah 6:5.

5. Isaiah had a specific reason for being scared. As he suddenly found himself in God's presence, he saw just how sinful he was. Point out that in the previous chapter, Isaiah had passed along six "woes" from God to various groups of people. Now he declares woe on himself. **Why do you think his focus was on his lips?** (The words that pass through our lips reveal thoughts or actions that are "unclean.")

6. Think about all of the words you've spoken during the past twenty-four hours. If you suddenly found yourself standing before God, realizing that He knew everything you'd said, would you feel OK? Or would you feel "unclean"? Explain.

7. What hope was there for Isaiah? If he was among the best of his people, and if *he* was ineligible to represent God, how is *anyone* able to (6:6, 7)? (We cannot live up to God's standards, but God can purify us from our sins.)

8. If you saw an angel flying toward you with a live coal aimed for your lips, what would you do? Why? Why do you think Isaiah didn't "duck and cover"? (He must have trusted God. After complaining about his lips, he seemed to know that God was going to deal with his complaint.)

9. As soon as Isaiah was cleansed by God, he became a willing servant, eager to do whatever God asked (6:8). Do you think the same is true of most people who become Christians today? Explain.

10. Isaiah's mission was to be an unusual one—he was to speak to people who weren't going to listen (6:9-13). If God knew they weren't going to listen, and if He had already planned to have their enemies take them into captivity, then why did He ask Isaiah to talk to them? (Everyone has a choice of whether or not to obey God. Even if God knows what we're going to choose, He doesn't remove the choice.)

11. Suppose God called you as His spokesperson to your school. What do you think would be His message? If you explained that God had personally appeared to you and had given you the message, do you think the people at school would listen? Why?

The reproducible sheet, "Lip Service," gives group members an opportunity to identify various body parts that might need to be purified before being put into service for God. After a few minutes, let volunteers share responses. Certainly, we need to be more aware of the words we speak (lips) as well as what we hear (ears) and see (eyes), where we go (feet), what we do (hands), and so forth. Explain that since all of God's people today are provided with spiritual gifts (I Corinthians 12:7), we *all* have a "calling." But perhaps, like Isaiah, we first need to be made aware of our own sinfulness and short-comings before we can be effective messengers for God. Close the session in prayer, asking God to help your kids see themselves more clearly and cleanse any and all of their "unclean" thoughts, words, and actions.

*Lip*SERVICE

Ring. Ring.

It's for you. You're receiving a call from God. He wants you to speak for Him and represent Him wherever you go. Are you ready?

No, we didn't think so. We suspected you might want to "touch up" a few things. Isaiah needed God's forgiving touch on his lips. So might you. But perhaps you want God to deal with some other areas as well before sending you out on a special mission for Him. So think about all of your recent thoughts and actions, and on the silhouette below, mark all of the areas that you would like God to cleanse before you feel worthy to be His representative.

ISAIAH 9

Baby Talk

Much of Isaiah's prophecy so far has been full of woe. The coming judgments of God are certain. However, Isaiah is just as certain that God will eventually forgive His people. More importantly, He will provide a very special means of forgiveness for them—a child who will be born to reign on David's throne and rule with justice and righteousness. God's current anger with His people is expressed in no uncertain terms, yet His promised Savior provides ongoing hope for them.

Hand out copies of the reproducible sheet, "Finders Keepers." The sheet will help group members see how much change can result from the sudden appearance of a baby in their lives. If your group members prefer activity to written assignments, roleplay some of the situations on the sheet using various sets of volunteers. Afterward, explain that as much as a "normal" baby tends to disrupt the established patterns of a person or family, the child described by Isaiah would establish lasting changes in the ways people lived.

DATE I USED THIS SESSION _____ GROUP I USED IT WITH _____

NOTES FOR NEXT TIME _____

_____

_____

1. Think of times in your life when you've been in the dark. When were you most thankful to have a light? Why? (Are there any cave explorers among your group members? Any people who have hiked through dark woods in the middle of the night? Any people whose cars have broken down on a moonless evening?)

2. On an emotional level, what kinds of things initiate "dark" moods for you? When you feel "in the dark" about something, what do you do to snap out of it?

3. Israel was an entire nation "in the dark," but God wanted them to know that one day they would see "a great light" (9:2). Obviously, He refers to the one we know to be Jesus. Would you say that people today are no longer in the dark? Why or why not? Almost two thousand years after Jesus' coming to earth, why do you think so many people are still in the dark spiritually? (The absence of Jesus in one's life results in darkness.)

4. Read Isaiah 9:1-5. **What do you think Isaiah is describing?** (Previous chapters have dealt with the inevitable defeat and captivity of God's people. Here Isaiah assures the people of eventual victory and an end to conflict.)

5. Ultimately, what will be the assurance of victory for God's people (9:6, 7)? (The coming of "a child"—the baby Jesus who would eventually rule "from that time on and forever.")

6. Jesus has several titles in Isaiah 9:6, 7. Be as specific as possible in explaining how Jesus is a "Wonderful Counselor." How is He a "Mighty God"? How is He an "Everlasting Father"? In what ways is He a "Prince of Peace"?

7. Of these four names, which means the most to you right now? Why? Which do you think you will most appreciate during the next year or so? Explain.

8. As soon as Isaiah inserts this wonderful promise in his writing, he goes back to the current state of his nation—which was sinful, evil, and headed for a fall. List all the

problems you find in Isaiah 9:8-21. (Pride and arrogance; desertion of God; false prophets; internal conflict; and so forth.) **How do the problems of Israel differ from the problems of our country today? Explain.**

9. **Three times in Isaiah 9 we read that God's "anger is not turned away, his hand is still upraised"** (9:12, 17, 21). **What do you think it takes to appease God's anger?** (All God desires from anyone is love and willing obedience to what He says. Of course, that may first require submission and repentance.)

10. **We aren't very different from the people of Isaiah's time. God expects us to be obedient to Him, and Christians have His assurance of something better to come— heaven. So why do you think more people aren't submissive? Do you think people today are better or worse than people in Isaiah's time? Explain.** (When we reject God today, we do so even though we have much more evidence of His love. Our awareness of what Jesus has done and the presence of the Holy Spirit should make us more willing to submit to God.)

11. **What's one thing you could do to be more submissive to God this week?**

(Needed: Materials to make signs)

It does little good to acknowledge God's greatness and love unless we experience it ourselves. So before kids leave, have each person make four signs, about bookmark size: (1) Jesus is a Wonderful Counselor; (2) Jesus is a Mighty God; (3) Jesus is an Everlasting Father; and (4) Jesus is the Prince of Peace. Challenge kids to rotate their signs on a daily basis, carrying one each day where they will see it frequently. Each time they see it, they should stop and think of one specific way in which Jesus is living up to that particular "name" in their lives. After a week of rotating their signs, you might want to have them memorize Isaiah 9:6 so they will "carry" Jesus' various titles with them on a more permanent basis.

FINDERS KEEPERS

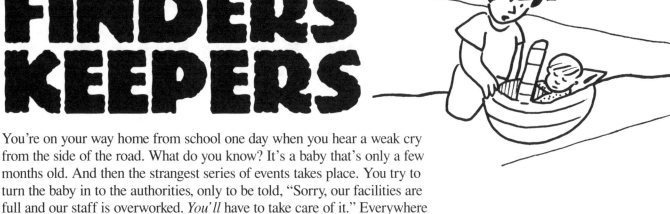

You're on your way home from school one day when you hear a weak cry from the side of the road. What do you know? It's a baby that's only a few months old. And then the strangest series of events takes place. You try to turn the baby in to the authorities, only to be told, "Sorry, our facilities are full and our staff is overworked. *You'll* have to take care of it." Everywhere you ask, you get the same answer. So you go home and explain to your parents that they have a new child, and they say, "Oh, no. We're much too busy to care for another child. It looks like this one is *your* responsibility."

From that moment on, you have an emotional "meter" in your head that ranges from "Ecstatic" at the top end to "Devastated" at the bottom. For each of the following events, determine where your meter would be.

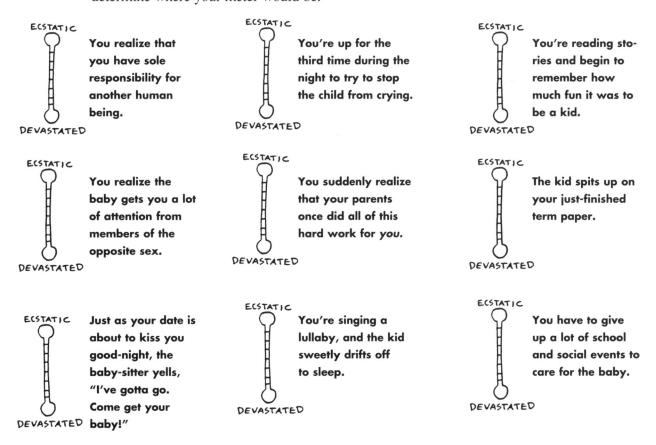

ECSTATIC — DEVASTATED

You realize that you have sole responsibility for another human being.

ECSTATIC — DEVASTATED

You're up for the third time during the night to try to stop the child from crying.

ECSTATIC — DEVASTATED

You're reading stories and begin to remember how much fun it was to be a kid.

ECSTATIC — DEVASTATED

You realize the baby gets you a lot of attention from members of the opposite sex.

ECSTATIC — DEVASTATED

You suddenly realize that your parents once did all of this hard work for *you*.

ECSTATIC — DEVASTATED

The kid spits up on your just-finished term paper.

ECSTATIC — DEVASTATED

Just as your date is about to kiss you good-night, the baby-sitter yells, "I've gotta go. Come get your baby!"

ECSTATIC — DEVASTATED

You're singing a lullaby, and the kid sweetly drifts off to sleep.

ECSTATIC — DEVASTATED

You have to give up a lot of school and social events to care for the baby.

After all of these things, would you keep trying to get someone to care for the kid, or do you think you might "get the hang of it" and decide to take care of it yourself? Explain.

ISAIAH 11–12

Branching Out

OVERVIEW

Isaiah predicts the coming of a future leader of Israel. But the Messiah, a "shoot . . . from the stump of Jesse," will not be like the leaders before Him. Rather, He will be godly, fair, and righteous. During His reign, even animals are described as living together in peace—including those that are usually natural enemies. In the meantime, God's people will be called out of captivity in various countries to reunite. The result will be praise and thanksgiving to God.

OPENING ACT

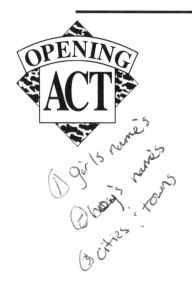

① girls names
② boys names
③ cities / towns

Begin the session with a game of Letter Link. Have kids sit in a circle. Choose a category (such as cities, girls' names, animals, song titles, etc.). The first person must name something that fits the category. After he or she has done so, the next person must think of something in the category that begins with the last letter of the previous word or phrase. So a series of cities might include Bosto__n__, __N__aple__s__, __S__an Francisc__o__, __O__ntario, and so forth. No answer may be repeated. Play until all but one person is eliminated. This activity can loosely symbolize the sequence of the kings of Israel. The common bond they were supposed to pass along was faithfulness to God, but few of the kings showed concern for God's wishes. David was one of Israel's greatest kings, but Isaiah predicts the coming of an even better leader from David's line.

DATE I USED THIS SESSION __1-28-07__ GROUP I USED IT WITH _____

NOTES FOR NEXT TIME_____

1. How much do you know about your ancestry? How far back can you trace your family tree? What was your original nationality? Do you have any noteworthy ancestors you know about?

2. Family and ancestry were of utmost importance in the Old Testament. For example, no one would have questioned Isaiah's reference to Jesse (11:1). But Jesse is not a recognizable name to some people today. What was important about him? (Essentially, he is remembered for being the father of King David.) If David was a lot more famous than Jesse, why wouldn't Isaiah refer to "the stump of David" instead? (As the father of David, Jesse would be honored as patriarch of David's descendants as well.)

3. Read Isaiah 11:1-5. What kind of ruler would this new leader be? Who do you think Isaiah is referring to? (Jesus, the Messiah.) Which of the qualities mentioned do you think is most important for a good leader?

4. Do you think Isaiah's prophecy has come to pass? Explain. (Some churches hold that Jesus has come as a servant, but not yet as king and ruler. See Isaiah 11:6-9 for additional hints that this period of time has not yet taken place. Other churches believe Christ is exercising a spiritual reign right now.)

5. What might a world be like that was "full of the knowledge of the Lord" (11:9)? How would such a world differ from the one you know?

6. What do you think Isaiah 11:10-16 is talking about? Explain. *world peace*

7. Since God cannot break a promise, what is something He has promised that you would like to affirm at this point in your life? Encourage group members to personalize biblical promises to solidify their faith.

8. Twice in Isaiah 12 the prophet uses the phrase "In that day you will say . . ." (12:1, 4). Then he describes the good things the people will say about God. But why might

these be perceived as sad statements? (Isaiah is saying that God will have to let His people be defeated and taken captive before they are reunited and become thankful to Him again.)

9. Do you tend to wait for exceptionally good things to happen before you think to praise God? Or are you more like the people of Israel, who refused to give God their loyalty until things got really bad for them? Explain.

10. What if, instead of waiting for something great to happen, we started every day by saying, *"Today* I will praise God and give thanks and sing"? Do you think your life would change? If so, in what ways?

The reproducible sheet, "Fast-Paced Praise Race," tests group members to see how quickly they respond when given an opportunity to praise God. Don't let anyone look at the sheet until you give a signal. At your signal, start a timer and let group members know exactly how much time they have. At your next signal, kids should put down their pencils. The person who wrote down the most answers is the winner of the race. But explain that everyone who includes praising God as part of each day's activities becomes more of a winner. If people had trouble thinking of things to put on their sheets, they may be out of practice. Challenge group members to focus on praise during the week to come, and see if it doesn't make a difference in their attitudes by the end of the week.

FAST-PACED Praise Race

This is a test to see who can come up with the most reasons to praise God. You may include as many answers as you can think of in each of the following categories. You get one point for every answer you record. But be warned: If someone challenges one of your answers, you must be able to defend it. (For example, you can't go through the phone book looking for names of people to be thankful for.) This is being timed, so don't dawdle. Use the back of the page if you need to.

What places are special to you, for which you should be thankful?

What things do you really like about yourself?

What enjoyable events take place only during this season of the year?

What people are you thankful for—not including relatives or members of this group?

What sounds do you think are really cool?

What are some things that you think smell wonderful?

What emotions do you appreciate because they make you feel strongly about things?

What wonders of creation have you witnessed during the past week?

What are some privileges you have because you live in a free country?

Who Do You Trust?

When the Assyrians seem like an overwhelming threat, Israel turns to Egypt as an ally rather than turning to God. God uses words like "obstinate," and "rebellious" to describe His people. The people have the same needs they've always had—comfort, security, protection, and such. But they have stopped turning to God to provide for those needs and are instead going to secular, sinful powers. Isaiah warns that God will eventually reveal His superior power—both to nations like Egypt and Assyria, and to His own people as well.

Have kids form teams for a Fireman's Carry Relay (in which two people interlock arms to carry a third person). All team members must participate in both carrying and being carried. So if there are four people on a team, Persons 1 and 2 would carry Person 3; Persons 2 and 3 would carry Person 4; Persons 3 and 4 would carry Person 1; and Persons 4 and 1 would carry Person 2. The people being carried must not touch the floor in any way; if they do, the team must begin again. The varying sizes of group members should cause challenges for some trios of people. If problems arise, use the opportunity to introduce the theme of the session: We should be careful about whom we rely on, because we may tend to put more faith in people and things than we should.

DATE I USED THIS SESSION _____ GROUP I USED IT WITH _____

NOTES FOR NEXT TIME _____

_____

_____

1. If you hear news that shocks you and makes you very upset, who's the first person you turn to? Why? Who do you call on if you get in trouble and need to be "bailed out"? Why? If a person or group is picking on you at school, who do you go to? Why?

2. God's people are supposed to rely on Him. But Isaiah points out that Israel was relying on the power of Egypt (30:1-5). **Why do you think the Israelites had switched loyalties?** (Sometimes people tend to put more trust in the things they can see rather than someone they can't see.)

3. God knew that Egypt's help to Israel would be "utterly useless" (30:7). **How did He try to tell His people** (30:10, 11)? (He sent prophets.) **Why didn't the people listen?** (They actually wanted the prophets to lie to them and tell them what they wanted to hear rather than the truth.)

4. In what ways do people today ignore the truth of God and still try to maintain some level of spirituality? (Some simply eliminate the portions of the truth that they find hard to accept, such as hell and judgment. Some mix Christian teachings with other, more "popular" philosophies.)

5. Ultimately, why do you think people don't believe *everything* God says—especially the parts they might not want to hear? (Perhaps they have it so good for so long that they stop wanting to deal with anything negative, even if it's the truth.)

6. What happens when we trust anything other than God to save us (30:12-17)? (When we choose to rely on something other than God, something stronger can always come along to threaten us again.)

7. When we suffer because of wrong decisions and bad alliances, do you suppose God ever thinks, *I told you so. Serves you right* (30:18-33)? **Explain.** (No. The Lord is gracious and promises to do wonderful things "as soon as he hears" our cries for help.)

8. Part of the solution to our problem is discovering that our "teachers will be hidden no more" (30:20). Do you agree that teachers of truth are often "hidden" from you? Explain. (Most of us are surrounded by an abundance of truth. However, sometimes we wish to pursue our own desires, so we hide *ourselves* from the truth and those who promote it [by dropping out of church, and so forth]. Yet if things get bad enough, we may be willing to return and let those people help straighten us out.)

9. What is always the problem of turning to other people or things rather than to God (31:1-3)? (People, regardless of size and number, are never as powerful as God. Physical possessions cannot compare to the spiritual help we need in times of crisis.)

10. It's clear to see that *Israel* should "return to him you have so greatly revolted against" (31:6). But what about *us*? Occasionally we get farther away from God than we intend to. So let's say God is in Topeka, Kansas. In the context of geographic location, where would you say you are in your relationship with Him? How might you begin to "return"?

The reproducible sheet, "Balancing Act," asks group members to label a number of things on which they depend for support. After a few minutes, ask volunteers to share their answers. Point out that it's fine to draw support from friends, family, and other sources, but not if it means ignoring what God has to say. The more "layers" we allow to come between ourselves and God, the less sure our footing will be in life. Close the session by having each group member think of one current source of support he or she uses that isn't a good one. Challenge the person to begin this week to let go of that source in order to get another step closer to God.

Most of us want God to support us in times of trouble. But the problem is that we aren't completely sure that God will come through for us, so we keep looking for additional sources of support. And we end up feeling much like the acrobat below.

Label each of his "supports" with one of the things you occasionally rely on. The things you depend on *most* should be at the bottom, with the less valid things toward the top. Try to include everything you lean on in times of stress, whether right or wrong—friends, family, sports activity, drugs and alcohol, money, pets, car, advice columns, horoscopes, books, stuffed animals, boyfriend/girlfriend, food, and so forth. When you finish, try to think of another circus analogy that illustrates what it would be like if you relied on God alone— without all of these other things. (Your head confidently in a lion's mouth? God's strong hands supporting you on the trapeze?)

ISAIAH 38–39

Not Dead Yet

The focus of Isaiah moves from the people in general to one of their kings in particular. King Hezekiah had been a good and godly king—a rare exception in the line of kings since Solomon. When God sends Isaiah to tell Hezekiah to prepare to die, the king pleads with God and receives an additional fifteen years of life—as well as an impressive sign from God. Yet Hezekiah certainly had his weaknesses, one of which was pride. After proudly showing off all of his possessions to visitors from Babylon, he is told that one day soon the Babylonians will haul it all off as their own.

Begin the session with roleplays. Using the reproducible sheet, "Second Chances," choose appropriate actors. Read each situation and let the performers act out what they think would happen. In each case, focus on what the person would do after being given a second chance. Would he or she try harder the second time? Make restitution for previous wrongs? Do exactly the same thing? Afterward, explain that we don't always get a second chance when we mess up, so we need to do as well as we possibly can the first time. Point out that in this session, kids will see that King Hezekiah got a second chance after being told he would die. Anyone who is "born again" should relate to his undeserved life extension.

DATE I USED THIS SESSION _____ GROUP I USED IT WITH _____

NOTES FOR NEXT TIME _____

_____

_____

1. Have you ever gotten a second chance to do something after you messed up the first time? If so, what were the circumstances? How did you do the second time?

2. Do you think God ever changes His mind? Explain. (Certain Bible verses indicate that God never changes. But if He is not influenced by prayers, why are we to pray and ask Him to act a particular way?)

3. Hezekiah was a good king of Judah, which was rare because most of the kings were wicked. But he received some disconcerting news, after which he hoped God would change His mind. What did he find out? See Isaiah 38:1. If you had gotten this news, what do you think would be the first three things you would do?

4. Hezekiah reminded God that he had spent his life being faithful, good, and wholeheartedly devoted to God (38:2, 3). Would you feel comfortable making the same claim? If not, what's keeping you from doing so?

5. God had originally told Hezekiah, "You are going to die; you will not recover" (38:1). But after Hezekiah prayed, God added fifteen years to his life (38:4-6). Do you think God changed His mind? Was God testing Hezekiah? What was the deal? Kids may have different opinions. But don't miss the point that, for whatever the reason, Hezekiah's prayer was involved in changing his gloomy situation.

6. If a prophet told you that you were certain to die, and then immediately changed his story, do you think you would be at all suspicious? How did God prove to Hezekiah that Isaiah was telling the truth (38:7, 8)? What signs do you have that God is at work in *your* life?

7. If you knew you were going to die soon, what would you give to have fifteen more years of life? Be specific. Hezekiah's life extension was a free and unexpected gift from God. What do you think would be an appropriate way to say thanks? (We may be accustomed to quick "thank yous" during our prayers, but Hezekiah left a detailed *written* record of what God had done for him [38:9-20].)

8. The news of Hezekiah's miraculous recovery spread far and wide. Soon he had visitors from Babylon—a powerful nation. How did Hezekiah treat his guests (39:1, 2)? Do you think his hospitality was appropriate, or perhaps a little excessive? Why? (The Babylonians were potential enemies of Israel, so Hezekiah shouldn't have been so accommodating.)

9. Isaiah, with God's knowledge of the future, knew exactly what was going to happen (39:3-8). What do you think about Hezekiah's reaction to the distressing prophecy that Judah would be looted by Babylon? (Hezekiah's response may seem self-centered, but perhaps he simply was accepting God's judgment without argument.)

10. Following Hezekiah's example, what is one request you would like to make of God even though you might not even dare think that He would grant it? Can you think of a disappointing circumstance that you feel God expects you to live with—trusting Him to get you through whatever it is? Why do you think God sometimes performs miraculous answers to prayer, and other times lets us suffer through undesired circumstances? (The contrast is not as vast as we might think. Whether granting incredible requests or seeing us through the most trying of times, God is demonstrating His grace to us.)

Point out that Hezekiah's grief at the news of his pending death was intense, so we might assume that he made the most of the fifteen additional years he received from God. Discuss as a group why it is that we so seldom appreciate life and all it contains until we are faced with losing it. Then, as a group, compile a list of "Ways to Start Living before You Start Dying." Begin with a few suggestions like play mud football more often, eat at a restaurant you know nothing about, go on a "date" with a close friend just for fun and not for romance, etc. Make the list as long as you can. Then have each person choose three things from the list to try during the week to come.

Second Chances

[Dear Leader: These are roleplays to help group members experience the sensation of receiving a second chance after a potentially devastating event. Read the set-up of each roleplay and let kids act out how they would feel and what they would do. Then stop them, read the "second chance" portion of the roleplay, and let them continue.]

1. For the first time ever, your school is in the state football finals. Luke, a wide receiver, has been one of the major reasons they've made it so far. He never drops a pass. Now, in the finals, your team is down by four points, but they're driving down the field. The ball is on the other team's 30-yard line, it's fourth down, and there's less than a minute on the clock. The quarterback takes the snap, drops back, sees Luke getting open in the end zone, throws a perfect pass right into Luke's arms in the end zone . . . and Luke drops it! The other team gets possession of the ball and needs only to run out the clock. [Have people play the roles of Luke, Luke's teammates, cheerleaders, spectators, and opposing team members. Their comments to each other should reveal their feelings.]

> **Second Chance:** There was a flag on the play. The other team was offside, so your team gets the down over again. The coach calls the exact same play. What do you think Luke will do this time? How do you think he feels?

2. Sina needs to ace her geometry exam in order to get a scholarship to Bratcliffe, an expensive college. The problem is that geometry was the last exam on her schedule, and by the time she got around to studying for the exam, she just didn't have any brain power left. Some of her friends came over who were celebrating because they were already finished with their exams, and Sina agreed to go out with them "for a while." She thought she would study when she got home, but that wasn't until after midnight, and she fell asleep instead. After taking the test, she knew as soon as she turned it in that she had really bombed. [Have people play the roles of Sina and her geometry teacher.]

> **Second Chance:** Later the teacher calls Sina aside and says, "Sina, I don't know what happened, but I seem to have lost your exam. I know you turned it in. Would you mind terribly if you took the test again tomorrow?" What do you think Sina might be thinking at this point? How do you think she'll spend her night?

3. Matty and Branford are good guys, but they were hanging around behind the shopping center one day when a lot of stuff got stolen. Several people are willing to testify to seeing them, and a lot of circumstantial evidence suggests that they are guilty. They were arrested, and a hearing is being held to see if they should go to trial. [Have people play the roles of Matty and Branford, as well as various people in the courtroom trial.]

> **Second Chance:** Someone announces that the actual thieves were caught and have confessed. How do you think Matty and Branford might react to the news? How do you think this incident will affect the way they spend their spare time from now on?

ISAIAH 40

Comfort and Hope

Isaiah has been clear in describing God's role as a judge who will soon "pass sentence" on His people and allow them to be overpowered by their enemies and taken into captivity. But now Isaiah reveals that God is also a God of comfort, who cares about the people. Even though they have been turning to worthless idols that cannot help them, God encourages the people to turn back to Him—the only one with the power to make a difference in their lives.

Have kids form teams. See which team can do the best job of making designated group members comfortable. Anything goes. Teams should yield the best seats to the designated people, get food or drink for them, and so forth. After a few minutes, talk to the people who were receiving comfort to see if you can determine which team did the best job of providing comfort. See if any of the teams went beyond *physical* means of comfort and began to try to deal with the emotional state of the people. Ask: **Can you truly be comfortable if you're worried about something?** Challenge kids to go beyond "expected" means of service and truly begin to care about other people's feelings and concerns. As God promised comfort to people, He tried to "set their minds at ease" to make sure they would have hope as well as physical comfort.

DATE I USED THIS SESSION _____ GROUP I USED IT WITH _____

NOTES FOR NEXT TIME _____

_____

_____

1. When you were a little kid, what special things did your parents do to comfort you after you had a nightmare or were otherwise upset? Now that you're older, do you miss those methods of comfort? Why or why not? These days, how do you seek comfort when you're upset? Why?

2. Previously Isaiah had described the Lord as a God of judgment. Now Isaiah reveals that the Lord is a God of comfort as well (40:1, 2). **How can God be both judging and comforting?** (Judgment of sin is necessary, but comfort is readily available after "sin has been paid for.")

3. Why do you think people usually need to be comforted (40:6-8)? (When we realize our human limitations [of both strength and length of life], we need assurance that everything will turn out OK.)

4. Why should we turn to God when we discover our limitations (40:9-14)? (God alone has the wisdom to know the future and the power to do what's best for us.)

5. Other than God, what things do people your age turn to for comfort? (Drinking, drugs, friends, sex, etc.) **On a scale of one to ten—with one being "worthless" and ten being "extremely effective"—how effective would you say each of these things are at providing lasting comfort?** See Isaiah 40:15-17. (The things we tend to value may be only "like a drop in a bucket.")

6. Would you say that any of the things you've listed qualify as *idols*? If so, in what ways? Compare group members' responses with Isaiah 40:18-20, which presents an image of people going to great lengths to build an idol that can't even stand up without a lot of help. Yet the people turn to that same idol in their search for peace and comfort.)

7. The description of God in Isaiah 40:21-27 sounds somewhat fierce. How are we supposed to find comfort from someone who "brings princes to naught and . . . blows on them and they wither, and a whirlwind sweeps them away like chaff" (40:23, 24)? (If God is not able to deal powerfully with sinful influences, His people cannot experience the comfort He promises.)

8. **We are told that no one can comprehend God entirely (40:28). Can you receive comfort from someone you don't understand? Explain.** (Little babies don't fully understand their parents, yet are comforted by them. Similarly, we will never fully understand God, yet we can know enough to trust Him.)

9. **We may tend to think of comfort in terms of gently swinging in a hammock with servants to fan us and feed us grapes. Do you think this is God's definition of comfort? If not, what do you think we should expect (40:28-31)?** (Comfort is finding the strength to keep going when we get tired or tripped up in some way.)

10. **Isaiah begins chapter 40 by discussing comfort and ends by talking about hope. Do you see a connection? If so, what is it?** (Hopeless people cannot be comforted. The goal of comfort is the promise [hope] that one's circumstances will get better.)

11. **What is one situation you're currently facing for which you could really use the comfort that only God can provide?**

The promises in the closing verses of Isaiah 40 are good ones to emphasize. The reproducible sheet, "The Great Right Hope," challenges group members to think of hope as a "product" that they can advertise and make appealing to other people. After a few minutes, let volunteers "pitch" their product to the rest of the group with a jingle, slogan, or whatever. Close the session with a prayer that God will keep reminding everyone that His hope is available at all times—especially in difficult and seemingly hopeless situations.

THE GREAT RIGHT HOPE

The management of Hope, Incorporated (whose slogan is "Hope Inc. for the Best") have come to you for help. They explain, "**KID, WE'VE COME TO YOU BECAUSE WE HEAR YOU'RE SHARP.** You're talented. You have a way of reaching people. And we like that. In fact, we pay big money for it. You see, we sell Hope. But our problem is that Hope is too intangible. You can't see it. You can't touch it. It's a hard thing to sell, kid, so we need your help. We want you to lay out an ad for us that will reach other kids your age. Make it so appealing that everyone will want to buy it. You can put it in any kind of package you want to, give it a snappy name, come up with a catchy jingle or slogan—anything you want to do. Just make Hope so irresistible to other people that they can't help but crave it. It's all up to you, kid. Our Hope is now in your hands."

So what do you think? Are you up to the challenge? Design the product and create your "sell copy" in the space below.

ISAIAH 42

Blind, Deaf, and Doomed

Due to years of disobedience, rebellion, and idolatry, God's people have become spiritually blind and deaf to His instructions. Consequently, they will be severely reprimanded as God allows their enemies to overpower them and take them into captivity. The nation of Israel was intended to be the servant of God, but simply hadn't gotten the job done. Therefore, God would send another special servant who would be completely obedient and would accomplish God's will on earth.

Use the reproducible sheet, "Job Interview," to introduce the topic of servanthood. Have three volunteers leave the room and then come in, one at a time, to apply for a job. Another person (the interviewer) should be given a copy of the reproducible sheet as a guideline for asking questions. As the expectations of servanthood become more specific and less pleasant, see where each volunteer "draws the line." Afterward, explain that the nation of Israel had stopped trying to be obedient to God. His requests were never unreasonable, yet the Israelites still refused to acknowledge Him.

DATE I USED THIS SESSION _____ GROUP I USED IT WITH _____

NOTES FOR NEXT TIME _____

_____

_____

1. What's the least pleasant work you've ever had to do? Why did you do it? How did you feel about it?

2. When you think of the word "servant," what other words come to mind? (If group members think in terms of people on the lower rungs of the socioeconomic ladder, they may resist becoming willing servants of God.) **If you were hiring your own personal servant, what chores would you expect him or her to do for you?**

3. If God were choosing a servant, what qualities do you think He would look for?

4. Who is the servant described in Isaiah 42:1-4? What makes you think so? (The qualities described strongly suggest that this is a messianic reference—that the servant is Jesus.)

5. Do the responsibilities of the person described here sound like things that would be assigned to a slave? Explain. (No. Being a servant of God is never a demeaning position. God's servants receive His Spirit and are empowered to do effective things—in this case, bringing justice and providing hope for others.)

6. Based on Isaiah 42:5-9, what would you say are some things God wants to do for us? (Take our hands, open our eyes, free captives, let us know what He's going to do, and so forth.) **Can you think of a specific way He has done one of these things for you lately?**

7. When God acts in our lives, He expects us to praise Him for it (42:10-17). When was the last time you spent more than three minutes thinking about how great God is or how much He has done for you? How do you think your life would be different if you decided to praise God for at least five minutes every day?

8. A recurring problem mentioned in Isaiah 42 is the issue of idolatry (42:8, 17). Do you ever struggle with idolatry in any form? Explain.

9. Do you think the servant described in Isaiah 42:18-20 is the same one referred to in verses 1-4? Explain. If it's not the same person, who do you think this one is? (The "servant" mentioned in Isaiah 42:19 is generally thought to be the nation of Israel. Compare Isaiah 41:8 and 49:3, where Israel is identified as God's servant.)

10. In what ways are God's servants today—Christians—occasionally "blind"? (We can experience so many things God does for us on a daily basis, yet take it all for granted and fail to give Him credit for it.) **In what ways might we be "deaf"?** (In spite of all of the Bible teaching and personal testimonies we hear, we can still tune it all out and choose to do what we want to do.)

11. According to Isaiah 42:21-25, what can people expect who remain blind and deaf to the things of God? (They are likely to be "plundered and looted" by others. And the tragedy is that even then they may not understand what's going on or turn to God for help.) **Can you think of any specific ways that people you know are suffering because they refuse to see or hear what God is doing for them? Explain.**

Close the session by asking group members to consider the question posed in Isaiah 42:23: "Which of you will listen to this or pay close attention in time to come?" Try to bring this chapter of Isaiah down to a very practical level. Ask: **How, specifically, can you become a better listener and pay closer attention to the things God wants you to know? How can you learn from the positive things God provides for you? How can you learn from the mistakes you make or the things that otherwise go wrong in your life?** After your group members come up with some specific ideas, go one step further and try to implement them. It's one thing to know you need to go to church more often to see and hear what God is doing; it's quite another to plan to get there and then commit yourself to the plan. Try to help your kids—as individuals and as a group—do whatever it takes to continue becoming the people God wants them to be.

Job Interview

[NOTE: In this skit, you will be interviewing a number of job applicants. The following script is just a guideline. Feel free to improvise as you wish.]

Mrs. Krinzkey, send in the next job applicant, please.

[Job applicant enters.]

Hello there. My name is Enmighty—Hy Enmighty. I'm the president of Intergalactic Gizmos Incorporated. And if you do well on this interview, you might just be the youngest vice president I've ever had. Say, I have this itch on my back I just can't reach. Would you mind scratching it for me? *[Give the specific location of the itch as the person scratches.]* What did you say your name was? *[Wait for response.]*

Don't be shy! Speak up, there. Tell me why you think you're better qualified for this job than anyone else. *[As the person answers, either encourage or discourage him or her with your facial expressions.]*

Well, it sounds like you have just the qualifications we're looking for. Tell you what, can you bring me that little paperweight? *[Point to a heavy object in the room and wait for the person to lug it over to you.]*

Thank you. Thank you. Say, you don't listen to that awful rap music, do you? No, I didn't think so. You don't look the type. Aw, shoot. There goes my arthritis. I get awful pains when the weather gets this way. If you don't mind, would you give my feet a good rubdown? I can't reach them anymore. They're farther away than they used to be. Don't be shy. Just rip those shoes off and don't let the sweat get to you. Sweaty feet are a sign of hard work, that's what I always say. *[Wait for the interviewee to give you a good foot massage.]*

That's it. Just keep it up while we talk. Tell me some of your hobbies. *[Wait for response.]*

OK. You can lay off the feet now. But I have to be honest with you. I'm interviewing a few other people for this job, so I'll get back to you. But first . . . *[Have the interviewee do any favor for you that you can think of.]*

Oh, one more thing—I got out of the house this morning before my spouse gave me my allowance. I'm getting powerfully hungry, and I could use a Big McWhopper and a jumbo order of Lard Fries. Do you have a couple of bucks on you that I could borrow until I see you next time? *[See how the person responds, then say good-bye.]*

ISAIAH 52:13–53:12

Weight on the Lord

Portions of the Book of Isaiah have dealt with the suffering God's people will have to endure because of their sins. This portion, however, details much of the suffering the Messiah will have to endure because of the sins of the people. This passage is quite specific about the things Jesus will eventually face at the hands of wicked and sinful people, as well as what He will receive from God after His selfless sacrifice.

Hand out copies of the reproducible sheet, "Unlikely Proposal." Give kids a few minutes to work on it. After everyone is finished, discuss kids' answers. See to what extent kids would be willing to suffer and/or embarrass themselves if they could get rich doing it. Then ask: **Of the things you agreed to do, how many would you still be willing to do if it provided one million dollars for *everyone else* in this group, but not you? In fact, the stipulation is that if anyone gives you any of the money, or any gifts bought with the money, the money is taken away from that person.** See which things kids would be willing to do for others if they didn't benefit personally. Tie in this discussion with the fact that Jesus' main purpose in His sacrificial death was not personal benefit. He did it purely for other people who were incapable of doing anything to deserve it or to pay Him back.

DATE I USED THIS SESSION _____ GROUP I USED IT WITH _____

NOTES FOR NEXT TIME _____

_____

_____

1. What's the most sacrificial thing you've ever se[en] someone do for someone else? (Donate a kidney; wor[k] make money for a brother or sister to go to college; etc.) you think you would do the same thing under similar circumstances? Why or why not?

2. In your opinion, why don't people act sacrificially toward others more often? (Perhaps they are afraid they won't receive as much support as they give.)

3. Chapters 52 and 53 of Isaiah describe God's "servant"—someone who acted sacrificially for everyone. In literature, such a person would be portrayed as a dashing hero. How is the Messiah described (52:13-15)? ("Disfigured," "marred beyond human likeness," and with an appearance causing others to be "appalled.") Do you think God could have had Jesus die for our sins without looking so terrible as He did it? If so, why didn't He? (Genuine sacrifice and death are hardly glamorous, no matter what images of heroes come out of Hollywood.)

4. In the Gospels we read about Jesus' being surrounded by people who wanted to see and touch Him. How can He be "despised and rejected by men, a man of sorrows, and familiar with suffering" (53:3)? (Many of the people He came to help were the very ones who had Him crucified.)

5. What does it mean to you that Jesus knows all about suffering and grief? (We should take comfort when we're facing unpleasant circumstances that Jesus knows *exactly* how we feel.)

6. According to Isaiah 53:4-6, Jesus carries our infirmities—the things we're too weak to do on our own; our sorrows—the emotional burdens we feel; and our transgressions and iniquities—the sins we commit. Give some examples of each of these things.

7. Jesus' death is compared to a lamb at a slaughterhouse (53:7). Can you think of one primary difference between Jesus' death and the slaughter of an animal? (Even though Jesus kept silent and appeared helpless, He wasn't. He could have avoided such a death if He so desired, but He was completely obedient to God's will and allowed Himself to be sacrificed out of love for us.)

8. **How do you feel when you see innocent people suffer at the hands of those who are stronger or more numerous? How do you think God felt to see Jesus put to death by sinful people? How do you think Jesus felt?** (No matter how Jesus felt, He prayed for the forgiveness of the people who killed Him.)

9. **Do you think Jesus got *anything* for dying for us? If so, what** (53:8-12)**?** (God rewards everyone who is obedient. Jesus was especially obedient, so He received "a portion among the great" [53:12]. Compare Philippians 2:8, 9 and Hebrews 2:9.)

10. **There is certainly no way to pay Jesus back for what He has done. Should we even try?** (Since Jesus died for us, we are to live for Him [II Corinthians 5:9, 14, 15]. He doesn't demand daily feats of faith that are next to impossible, yet He does expect our love and obedience.) **What is one thing you've done for Jesus today?**

If it hasn't come out in the discussion so far, emphasize the fact that Jesus' sacrifice was *voluntary.* Certainly, it was God's will, yet Jesus needed no prodding or coercion to sacrifice Himself. Have group members use percentages to estimate how much of their Christian growth and service takes place because they do it on their own, and how much is due to the pressure of parents, pastors, youth group leaders, or others. Then discuss ways that group members can increase the percentage in the first category as they lower the latter percentage. Close with a prayer of thanksgiving for the weight God carries for all of us. Ask God for courage for your group members to become more willing to share the weights that other people may be carrying.

UNlikely Proposal

Not long ago, a movie titled *Indecent Proposal* had people talking about whether or not they would allow a spouse to sleep with a stranger for one million dollars. The possibility of "easy money" is an allurement to many people. While not all people would compromise their moral standards just to get rich, they might have other things they would be willing to do. Check the boxes of the things that you would be willing to do for the designated amount.

What Would You Do for $1,000,000?

❏ Go to prison—with hardened criminals— for a year

❏ Work as a sewer scuba diver for the next 20 years

❏ Do without all sweets for the rest of your life

❏ Donate a kidney to a stranger who needs it

❏ Participate in a scientific experiment in which you have horrible nightmares all night—every night—for six months

❏ Get a full-body tattoo, allowing the "artist" to choose which images to use

❏ Live on an island for two years where you will be comfortable, but will have absolutely no contact with other human beings

What Would You Do for $100?

❏ Shave your head

❏ Sing "1,000 Bottles of Beer on the Wall" all the way down to zero—nonstop

❏ Eat a fried earthworm sandwich using no less than 25 earthworms

❏ Use a wheelchair for an entire week anytime you want to go somewhere

❏ Walk into your local public pool wearing your underwear instead of a swimsuit

❏ Go on a date with someone you really like with a big hunk of spinach between your front teeth

❏ Do without TV, movies, or music for a month

What Would You Do for $10?

❏ Eat a bug of your choice

❏ Do 500 situps

❏ Do everything your parents tell you to do for an entire day

❏ Read *War and Peace*

❏ Stay awake for 72 hours straight

❏ Drink a case of root beer in less than one hour

❏ Go on a date with someone you can't stand

ISAIAH 55

The World's #1 Thirst Quencher

In a tender and personal appeal, God encourages "thirsty" people to "come to the waters." This message is directed to the people who would go into exile and would be eventually called back into God's favor. Yet its appeal is also to anyone who hungers and thirsts for righteousness (Matthew 5:6).

(Needed: Food)

Have kids form teams. Conduct a relay to see which team can eat the most thirst-producing foods in a given period of time. For example, the first person on each team might run to the food table and eat a cupful of salty peanuts. Then that person would run back to tag the second person on the team, who must also eat a cupful of peanuts. When the entire team has eaten the first course, move on to other ones: a peanut-butter sandwich, extremely dry cake, a whole jalapeño pepper, etc. At the completion of the relay, begin the meeting immediately—without opportunity for a water break. See what happens when thirst becomes a priority. Can most kids focus on spiritual things, or must their thirst first be quenched?

DATE I USED THIS SESSION _____ GROUP I USED IT WITH _____

NOTES FOR NEXT TIME _____

_____

_____

1. What's the thirstiest you can ever remember being? What were the circumstances? How did it feel when you finally drank something?

2. We know that God is the owner and landlord of everything on earth. How would you feel if He let you enjoy all of the privileges of life, but only if you paid a high rent every month?

3. God's provision for us is "without money and without cost" (55:1). **Does that mean we don't owe God anything? Explain.** (We owe God everything. Just because He doesn't demand payment doesn't mean we shouldn't give ourselves to Him willingly.)

4. What are some things young people spend money on that "[do] not satisfy" (55:2)? Why do you think so much money is spent on makeup, music, cars, dates, and such, when so little is given to the church or otherwise devoted to spiritual things?

5. What are some things we can expect if we devote ourselves and our possessions to God (55:1-5)? (Some of the things mentioned include an enriched and delighted soul, wisdom and leadership, God's love, and splendor.) **How, specifically, do you think people receive such things?** (Perhaps they receive peace during trying times. Perhaps they earn the respect of a few conscientious people, if not big crowds. Perhaps they have a satisfaction with life, even though they may not have a lot of money.)

6. What do you think it means to "seek the Lord while he may be found" (55:6)? (God certainly isn't going to go away, but the danger lies in hardening our hearts to Him until *we* lose interest.) **How do we "find" God (55:7)?** (We must respond to Him by repenting of our wrongdoing and turning to Him.)

7. If we concede that God is much smarter than we are, and that His ways and thoughts are higher than ours (55:8, 9), then why do you think we sometimes challenge what He says to do? Why do we presume to know better?

8. Have you ever spoken up for God and been laughed at or otherwise rejected? How did you feel? According to Isaiah 55:10, 11, do you think you should regret the experience? (No. Perhaps the message was simply "rain" in the life of the other person, and will *eventually* result in something positive.)

9. Sometimes we speak of "suffering for the Lord." Do you think God wants us to have an attitude of suffering and martyrdom because we believe in Him? See Isaiah 55:12, 13. (Though we may suffer on occasion, we should be filled with joy and peace.)

10. After you find your way to God's "waters," what kinds of things can you do to help other thirsty people find their way to His spring?

Conclude the session with the reproducible sheet, "Thought Control." Cut apart the situations listed on the sheet. One at a time, give a situation to a volunteer who should read it and *immediately* give his or her thoughts on the matter—his or her instinctive, gut reaction to the situation. Then, as a group, try to think of what God's thoughts might be on the matter. Since God's thoughts are much higher than our thoughts, God might desire us to act differently in many of the given situations.

Challenge group members to pay careful attention during the next week to *actual* situations that come up. Each person should describe at least one such incident at your next meeting to see how other group members might have responded. If you can help group members recognize the situations in which they have a choice to make, the actual making of the decision becomes much easier.

Thought CONTROL

1. You're with a date at a very nice, expensive restaurant. But while you're trying to enjoy your meal and a little intimate conversation, the people at the next table, who are about your age, are getting more and more rowdy. You notice that they've brought their own flasks of something that's making them very drunk. You try your best to ignore them, but just after your entrée is served, one of them stands to "Proposh a toasht," and topples in a drunken stupor right across your table, sending your meals crashing to the floor. What would you do? What are your thoughts toward your fellow diners?

2. On a curvy back road, you get stuck driving behind some old person who's doing about 20 in a 50 m.p.h. speed zone. But you can't safely pass because of the hills and curves. At last, you get to a straight stretch with no traffic coming, and the person practically comes to a stop. You go for it, attempting to pass, and the person turns left right into you. No one is hurt, but as the police write up the accident, *you* are ticketed for reckless driving. (The old person says she signaled to turn left, but you never saw it.) What, if anything, would you do about your ticket? What are your thoughts toward the old person? Toward the police?

3. A teacher has a "pet" in your history class, and it sure isn't you. You've tried all year to make A's in the class, but simply can't do it. Still, you do a lot better than "teacher's pet" because you and she compare grades after every test. Yet at the end of the term, she has an A and you have a B. You ask, "How can this be?" She says, "Oh, the teacher let me do some 'extra credit' assignments to get my grade up." You know for a fact that nobody else was offered an opportunity for extra credit. What would you do? What are your thoughts toward your fellow student? Toward the teacher?

4. A homeless guy stops you and a friend as you're going down the street. As your friend is looking for some spare change, the guy throws up and gets a little on one of your shoes. What would you do? How would you feel about the guy?

5. Your best friend has a ten-year-old sister who has leukemia. You and the entire youth group have regular prayer vigils for the girl, asking God to heal her. But after almost a year of faithful prayer, she dies. What do you think you would do upon hearing the news of her death? How would you feel toward God?

ISAIAH 60

Got a Light?

OVERVIEW

Using the symbolism of darkness and light, God (through Isaiah) tells of a better time to come after Israel's eventual exile. The return of God's favor is portrayed as a great light upon the nation that will not only change the people's own status, but will also attract others. The symbolism becomes reality in God's eternal kingdom, where we will have no need for sun or moon since God Himself will be the light.

OPENING ACT

(Needed: Candles, matches)

Make the room as dark as possible. Have kids form two teams. Give each person a candle. Line up one team against a wall and the other team against a perpendicular wall. Light the candle of one person on each team. The goal is for all team members to light their candles and move to the opposite wall of the room. The catch is that people can move only while their candles are burning. If a candle goes out for any reason, whether blown by the wind or extinguished by a person on the other team, the person with the unlit candle must freeze until it is relit by a team member with a burning candle. The first team to successfully get all of its members across the room with lit candles is the winner.

DATE I USED THIS SESSION _____ GROUP I USED IT WITH _____

NOTES FOR NEXT TIME _____

_____

_____

1. Have you ever awakened at three or four in the morning, perhaps when you were sick or camping out, and just couldn't seem to get back to sleep? How did you feel as you sat there, just waiting for morning to come? How did you feel when you finally saw the first rays of the sun breaking through the darkness?

2. Isaiah has been describing a "dark" time coming for the people of Israel—their capture by, and exile to, foreign countries. How would you feel if you were suddenly attacked by a foreign country, captured, and carried off to that country for what could be the rest of your life?

3. To make things worse, the people of Israel would know that their capture was directly related to their sin and refusal to turn to God when they had the opportunity. If you were in such a situation, what would you do? (The situation would be likely to cause people to either turn back to God for help, or become more angry and stubborn as they continued to reject Him.)

4. When you experience physical, emotional, or spiritual darkness, what do you think God wants you to know (60:1, 2)? (God is a glorious light who can disperse the darkness when we allow Him to.)

5. How may ways can you think of in which God acts as light? (He can "enlighten" people who need wisdom. He can "light the path" of those who need direction in life. He can "light a fire" under people without energy or passion. He can provide new ideas for problems—provide the "light bulb" that appears over the person's head, so to speak.)

6. When you've been in darkness for a long time, and suddenly begin to experience the light of God in your life, how might that affect other people (60:3-16)? (If we are true to God, other people may be impressed and influenced by what He can do for and through us.)

7. What do you think Isaiah 60:17 is talking about? (It's usually not hard to see situations in which we've chosen to do evil rather than to obey God. But sometimes it's more difficult to see situations in which we've chosen something that's good, but where God has something better to offer.) **Can you think of an example in which you may seem to be doing OK, but where God might show you an even better way to handle the situation?**

8. Name a situation for which you need God to shed some light on the matter and help you make the best possible decision or solve a hard problem. According to Isaiah 60:18-22, how long can you expect God's wisdom to work for you? (God's light is everlasting. We need His ongoing help and wisdom.)

9. Isaiah promises that "your days of sorrow will end" (60:20). **Do you really believe that you won't have any sorrow as long as your faith in God is strong? Explain.** (Certainly faith helps get us through our times of sorrow, but unpleasant circumstances are certain to continue to occur. Isaiah's prophecy is more long-range. Once we get to heaven where sin has been eliminated and God is completely in charge, there will be no more sorrow.)

10. Of all of the things we're told we can expect in Isaiah 60, which single promise seems most relevant to you at this time in your life? Why?

The reproducible sheet, "Be Truthful to Your School," gives kids a sense of what it must have been like to be a prophet. Even though Isaiah was bringing good news in Chapter 60, it was only after he told the Israelites about a lot of bad things that would first occur. After a few minutes, ask a few volunteers to read what they've written. Then spend some time discussing what it would be like to confront people—friends, perhaps—about the sins they commit. Also discuss how your group members can receive the good things of God without going through a lot of bad stuff first. Challenge each person to *voluntarily* turn away from personal sins and shortcomings before God takes action. It is possible to receive the blessings of God without first experiencing His judgment, but we must make some hard decisions before such a thing is possible.

BE <u>Truthful</u> TO YOUR SCHOOL

Isaiah was a prophet during the dark days prior to the exile of Israel. He had the duty of telling the Israelites about the bad things that were going to happen first, and then about the good things to come after the bad things had taken place. Imagine you're a prophet at a dark place—your school. You probably already know about the bad stuff. But you might need to warn fellow students about the consequences of some of their sinful activities, as well as what is in store for whoever is faithful to God. So get to work on your prophecy. You can start your first rough draft below.

The Book of _____

(Your name here)

This is the message of _____, a servant of God, to the people at the dark

place called _____ (and the darkest of all places *within*

that place: _____). The way I see it, you guys have a choice.

You can either shape up and stop all of that _____

you've been doing, or else you can just keep going. But I have to warn you, if you don't

stop, I wouldn't be surprised if God _____. After all,

He can't tolerate intentional sin. Your future will be _____ and your pre-

sent circumstances will soon become _____.

But if you decide to shape up, turn to Him, and act the way He wants you to, you will

see a difference. Your grades will _____, you will discover a brand new

_____, and your whole life will become _____. I know the

hardest thing for most of you to do will be to give up _____ and start to

_____. But you can do it. And after all of the immediate benefits

of turning to God, an even better long-range result is _____.

If you guys believe me, I hope you'll change and see for yourselves what a difference

God can make in your lives. If you don't believe me, I just hope you won't take me and

_____.

JEREMIAH 1

Jeremiah Was a Bronze Wall

When Jeremiah is called by God, his response is similar to Isaiah's (Isaiah 6)—he feels unworthy and reluctant to speak for God. But God cleanses Jeremiah and assures him that the words will be provided for him to pass along to God's people.

Hand out copies of the reproducible sheet, "Secret Agent Kid." Say: **On the old TV show "Mission: Impossible," each episode would open with a secret agent looking through dossiers that showed other agents' special strengths and qualifications. He then chose the people who would be best for the mission. You may not know this, but I'm a secret agent as well. And in an attempt to recruit some of the finest young minds in the country, I would like to assemble dossiers on all of you. Please cooperate by filling out the information requested on this sheet.** After a few minutes, have group members discuss how they would feel to be chosen for a special mission for their country. Some may feel that such a job would be too much at this stage in their lives. If so, help them relate to Jeremiah, who felt like "only a child" when God called him to be a prophet.

DATE I USED THIS SESSION _9-17-06_ GROUP I USED IT WITH _Sunday School_

NOTES FOR NEXT TIME _____

_____

_____

1. What are some things that people say you're still "too young" to do? (Perhaps drive, vote, stay home alone, set your own curfew, get a job, etc.) **If given an opportunity, do you think you'd be just as good at those things as anyone else?**

2. **At church, do you have limitations on what you can and can't do because of your age? At what age do you think it's your responsibility to start tithing regularly, participating on church committees, going to church business meetings, and so forth? Explain.**

3. **When God first told Jeremiah to be a prophet, Jeremiah reasoned that he was "only a child"** (1:6). **Yet he was already a priest** (1:1). **What do you think would be the main differences between a priest and a prophet?** (Men born in the line of Levi had a right to serve as priests, and they had an established job description. To greatly oversimplify—priests sacrificed and prophets spoke out. Prophets were usually more isolated and were perceived as confrontational. It would probably be easier to be a priest than a prophet during this time.)

4. **When did God decide that Jeremiah would make a good prophet** (1:1-5)? (God created him to be a prophet.) **Do you think God could have some kind of similar calling in mind for you? Explain.**

5. **When Jeremiah tried to claim that he was "only a child," what did God do** (1:6-10)? (God confirmed and empowered Jeremiah.) **What is one thing you think God might be willing to empower you to do—if you agreed to it?**

6. **How could Jeremiah be sure that God was going to use him** (1:11-16)? (God began right away to show Jeremiah visions and explain them to him.) **Have you detected any signs recently that God might want you to do something specific with your life?** Point out that signs can be as simple as strong interests and skills in a particular area.

7. **It must have been kind of exciting to be singled out to**

speak for God. Do you think Jeremiah was excited? Explain. (The first news Jeremiah received was bad. His country was going to be judged by God and overpowered by its enemies.)

8. **How good are you at telling other people news they don't really want to hear? Would the message God wanted you to present affect your willingness to be a prophet? Explain.** (At various places in the Bible, God condemned prophets who told people only what they wanted to hear. We need to deal with truth, no matter how unpleasant that truth might be.)

9. **Do you think God might have sensed some reluctance in Jeremiah** (1:17-19)**?** (God gave Jeremiah a "pep talk" to give him confidence.)

10. **Do you think God's promise to make Jeremiah "a fortified city, an iron pillar and a bronze wall" was just for the prophet? Or is it symbolic for anyone who takes a stand for God? Explain.**

– confident

11. **If you felt more "fortified," what might you attempt for God that you've been a little hesitant to do until now?**

(Needed: An assortment of objects, a bag)

The use of symbolic language in prophecy is occasionally confusing, but it has benefits as well. For example, when we say God makes us strong, the truth of the statement may or may not sink in. But when God calls someone an iron pillar, for example, we know exactly what kind of strength He's talking about. Put an assortment of objects in a bag. Pass the bag around. Have each person reach in, pull out the first object he or she touches, and make a spiritual comparison using the object. For example, if someone pulls out an eraser, he or she might say, "This eraser symbolizes God because He is always ready to wipe out my sins when I confess them to Him." Close with a prayer of praise to God, who is so complete that He can make us complete in every way as well.

Secret Agent Kid

NAME:

CODE NAME YOU WOULD LIKE TO GO BY—AND WHY:

SPECIAL SKILLS:
(These need not be spying skills; they can be anything you do well.)

WEAKNESSES:
(These may include vision problems, allergies, medical concerns, phobias, etc.)

PERSON(S) IN THE GROUP YOU WORK BEST WITH:

PLACE(S) YOU COULD INFILTRATE THAT OTHER PEOPLE YOUR AGE CAN'T:

IF YOU ARE CAUGHT OR CAPTURED, WHO CAN BE CONTACTED WHO KNOWS ALMOST ALL OF YOUR SECRETS?

IMITATIONS OR IMPERSONATIONS YOU CAN DO:

ODD, QUIRKY TALENTS YOU HAVE THAT FEW OTHER PEOPLE DO:

JEREMIAH 2–4

So What's the Good News?

Jeremiah's message to Judah is not good. God feels as if His people have jilted Him like a wife who has left her husband. At one time the relationship had been strong, but the people have forsaken God for other idols and their own selfish interests. Consequently, God tells of disaster that will come from the north—the enemies of Judah will overpower the people and destroy life as they know it.

Play "The Divorce Game" (which is similar to the old TV game show "The Newlywed Game"). Recruit three couples who supposedly hope to get a divorce. You'll also need a person to ask questions of the three couples. Explain that only one of the three couples will be granted the divorce they seek, and it's up to the person asking the questions to determine which marriage has the most problems. In a competition like this, problems are likely to be exaggerated and conflict intensified. After the person makes his or her decision, point out how quickly two people can turn on each other. Explain that a divorce analogy is used in this session to show how God feels about the way Judah deserted Him to pursue other gods.

DATE I USED THIS SESSION _____ GROUP I USED IT WITH _____

NOTES FOR NEXT TIME _____

_____

_____

1. Have you ever been close friends with someone, but eventually realized that the two of you didn't have a lot in common and should probably spend your time pursuing other relationships? If so, did the relationship just drift apart, or did one of you say, "I'd like to spend more time with other people"?

2. On a scale of one to ten—with one being "terrible" and ten being "extremely good"—how good do you think you are at passing along bad news to other people with the least amount of shock or hurt feelings on their part? How good are you at *receiving* bad news?

3. Jeremiah had a lot of things to tell the people of Israel—things that they didn't want to hear. He started with a short history lesson. **What had God done for His people in the past** (2:1-8)? (He had delivered them from Egypt to the promised land and had given them the best of everything.) **What has God done for *you* lately?** (If we see clearly the things that God does in our lives, we aren't so likely to complain that God isn't around when we need Him.)

4. God accuses the people of making idols, worshiping the idols, failing to be comforted by the idols, and then blaming *Him*—the real God—when things went wrong (2:11-13, 27-29). **Do you think people do the same kind of thing today? If so, in what ways?** (People may put their faith in friends, money, and so forth. Then, when those things let them down, the people accuse God of deserting them when they have actually deserted Him.)

5. The people of Israel seemed to think that because God had not yet taken severe action against them, whatever they were doing must be OK (2:32-35). **Do you think some people today have similar attitudes? Explain.** (Many people try to establish a direct connection between good or bad circumstances and their current status with God. We need to develop a consistently godly lifestyle, regardless of what happens to us.)

6. God compares His people to animals in heat (2:23-25) as well as to an unfaithful wife guilty of prostitution (3:1-

5). **If you had a spouse who left you to sleep around with all kinds of other people, what emotions would you feel? Do you think God actually feels those emotions as well?** (Since His love is more perfect than ours, He feels more strongly than we do about being betrayed and forsaken.)

7. **The nation of Israel had already been defeated by the Assyrians for exactly the same things that Judah was now doing wrong** (3:6-10). **The people of Judah saw what happened to Israel, but didn't change the things they were doing wrong. How might this apply to people today?** (Many people see the tragic consequences of a non-Christian lifestyle, yet refuse to change their own sinful actions.)

8. **What do you think God wants of His people, anyway** (3:11–4:4)**?** (We may think in terms of rules and regulations, but God is eager to restore a loving and giving *relationship* if we will only turn to Him and place Him first in our lives.)

9. **Specifically, what was about to happen because of Judah's unfaithfulness** (4:5-31)**?** (Nations from the north would conquer Judah.) **Specifically, what might you expect to happen to people today who remain unfaithful to God?**

10. **What are some ways to keep from becoming indifferent to the priorities of God?**

The reproducible sheet, "This . . . Is BNN," contains a skit. Assign parts to volunteers and let them present the skit. Afterward, discuss the similarities and differences between our country and the nation of Judah. Which of the same problems do we have? How, if anything, are we more responsive to God than they were? Explain that while we sometimes can't affect the national attitudes and laws the way we might wish to, we can *always* take responsibility for our personal actions and attitudes. That's where positive change begins— in the lives of individuals. Close the session by asking God to begin working in the lives of your individual group members, then in your group as a whole, then in your church, and on from there.

This Is . . . BNN

NARRATOR: It's eight o'clock, and this is BNN, your twenty-four-hour Bad News Network. This segment is brought to you by Bower's Aspirin, Preparation Ouch—for when those hemorrhoids just won't go away, A-Tisket A-Casket Mortuary Service, and Federal Excuse—when your package absolutely positively didn't get there on time. Now here are your co-anchors: Todd Toddy and Tiffany Troutman.

TIFFANY: Good evening. This . . . is BNN! Our top story tonight: Hordes of Babylonian troops have been sighted assembling just across our northern border all day today. No one will comment on this gathering, but it looks bad, so we're reporting it. Todd?

TODD: Thanks, Tiff. In our BNN exclusive, we continue to report on the disrepair of our national shrines. Our all-powerful warrior god, Biff, was found face down in a pile of ox . . . well, let's just say "ox mud." Our honored idols all across Judah need work—resculpturing, repair from termite damage, new gold plating, and so forth. People have begun to complain that if they're going to put so much faith in these divine entities, they want their little wooden-headed gods to look a lot better. Now let's check in with Jock Trap for the sports.

JOCK: What do you expect from a Bad News Network, Todd? In football, Babylon Headbangers, 56; Judah Kitty Cats, 3. In baseball, the Assyrian Annihilators, 13; Jerusalem Jackrabbits, 0. In basketball, the Nineveh Wild Wolves skinned the Judah Little Lambs by a score of 126 to 43. And in ice hockey, well, there's still no ice around here, so the game was again canceled. Back to you, Tiffany.

TIFFANY: Thanks, Jock. This just in: A woman has been found in the temple courtyards. It seems that she may have been there for weeks, after a stroke had incapacitated her. She's being treated at Jerusalem General.

TODD: Hey, that's the best news we've had on this station in a long time. Not that she was hurt, of course, but that someone found her. I mean, who goes to the temple these days? Now let's go to Storm Cummings for the weather. Storm?

STORM: No change, Todd. Through the whole viewing area we've got heat. We've got drought. We've got locusts. We've got lousy, stinking—

TODD: Thanks, Storm, but our time is up. So for the Bad News Network, this is Todd Toddy . . .

TIFFANY: And Tiffany Troutman, saying . . .

TODD & TIFFANY: When it comes to bad news, you'll hear it here first.

JEREMIAH 7

Lack of Truth— and Consequences

OVERVIEW

God challenges the false religion of the people of Judah. He makes it clear that simply going to the temple on a regular basis is not a sign of a healthy religion. He calls on the people to change their ways and actions, but realizes that they won't. Therefore, He says that He is going to pour out His anger and wrath on the people. As a result, the valley where the people now go to offer their children in fiery sacrifices to other gods will soon be called the Valley of Slaughter and become a cemetery where Babylonian invaders will kill the people of Judah. The dead will be buried "until there is no more room."

OPENING ACT

Make a mental note of the things you hear kids talking about before the meeting. Begin the session with the skit on the reproducible sheet, "Grating Greetings." Give one person a copy of the sheet. That person should pretend to be sitting on the church steps. Kids should walk by as if entering church, while this person makes comments from the sheet. Afterward, discuss how kids would feel about being confronted in such a manner, even if the accusations were true. Then point out that God gave Jeremiah this very job of confronting people.

DATE I USED THIS SESSION _____ GROUP I USED IT WITH _____

NOTES FOR NEXT TIME _____

_____

_____

1. **Why do you go to church? List all of the reasons you can think of.** (If kids are honest, many should admit that social opportunities and being forced by parents frequently take priority over a sincere desire to worship God.)

2. Mention some of the things you overheard group members talking about before the session. **Did you come here today to talk about these things? Or did you come for spiritual enrichment? If you had a choice, what would you talk about during the next hour?** (While things such as friends, music, school, and such are important, none should be allowed to interfere with spiritual growth.)

3. **Jeremiah did what God told him to do** (7:1, 2). **When you know that some of your Christian friends are doing things that aren't right, do you tend to confront them or to look the other way? What determines your actions?**

4. **The people believed that going to the temple would make them OK with God, and that then they could behave as they wished** (7:3-8). **But what did God expect of them rather than simply going to church?** (Compassion for strangers, orphans, and widows; peace; faithfulness to God; etc.) **What actions do you think God expects of *us* to indicate that our faith is sincere?**

5. **God knew that the people who came to "worship" were active thieves, murderers, adulterers, liars, and worse** (7:9-11). **What do you think are some of the most common unconfessed sins among people who pose as good churchgoing Christians today?** (Perhaps gossip, getting rich by taking financial advantage of others and then giving a small amount in the offering, apathy toward God, etc.)

6. **On a scale of one to ten, to what extent would you say churches today serve as dens or hideouts for people who don't really want to stop sinning, yet want to try to make themselves look good? To what extent would you say this is true of *our* church?**

7. **What was one reason the falling away from God was so widespread in Judah** (7:16-19)? (Parents were getting children involved in the worship of other gods.) **Do you tend to go along with what your parents say about God, or do you check things out for yourself? Explain.**

8. **God knew that the people were too far gone to be persuaded by anything less than a catastrophe to turn back to Him** (7:20-29). **So why do you think He sent Jeremiah with this message anyway?** (Perhaps after the invasion of Babylon, the people would remember that God had at least tried to warn them.)

9. **Do you think God is being too hard on His people when He allows vicious armies to roll in and slaughter them in huge numbers** (7:30-34)? **Explain.** (The people were sacrificing their own children to other gods. It's hard to blame God for allowing them to die when they had become willing to kill each other.)

10. **Suppose a 100-story building represents your spiritual potential. The top floor symbolizes spiritual perfection. The basement is as low as you can go. On what floor is your elevator right now? What's the highest you've ever been? What do you think you need to do to keep moving up instead of down?**

It's relatively easy to look back at a sinful nation and think, *Oh, how terrible that they wouldn't quit sinning and just start obeying God.* Yet even while we're thinking it, we may be overlooking the things that are wrong in our own lives. Spend the final minutes of the session devising a "Plan to Stop 'Backsliding' and Start Growing." Start with the things your group members have learned from Jeremiah 7: don't overlook sin; recognize idols for what they are; don't let truth perish; etc. Add anything else you can think of. After brainstorming ideas, organize them into a plan your group members can put into practice. Then make copies of the plan and hand them out to everyone at your next meeting.

Grating Greetings

[Dear Volunteer: This is a skit, but you're the only person with a script. You're supposed to be a modern-day prophet on the steps of your church. As people enter, select appropriate comments from the ones listed below. After you get the hang of it, feel free to add "greetings" of your own. Just be sure you don't use real names and situations, or get too personal. This is supposed to be fun.]

Good morning, Juan. I'm surprised to see you here today after seeing how drunk you got at the party last night.

Hi there, Byron. Good to see you and your lovely wife, Carla. She's almost as lovely as that girl you were out with last night.

Well, if it isn't Mr. What-Uncle-Sam-doesn't-know-won't-hurt-him. My Dad is the guy who does your taxes, and he talks in his sleep. I'd better tell the church treasurer to double check the math on your giving envelope.

Hi, Sarah. I hear from Suji who heard from Debbie who heard from Jose's sister who heard from her hair stylist who heard from her mailman that you're a bit of a gossip.

Hello, Don Marchelloni. I know you kept it hidden from the Rosati family, but I know you made hits on six of their "family" last week. Welcome to church.

And here's Mrs. Needmore, my old boss who fired me along with about a dozen other people. I just found out you replaced us all with illegal aliens who work for half minimum wage and don't get benefits. You have a good worship service, you hear?

Ah, it's Dan. I had the usher save you a good seat in the back so you can sneak out early and make sure you don't miss the kickoff. Exactly what is it you're worshiping there, Dan?

It's Lyle. Every day at school you have a new racist joke to tell. Maybe you'd like to share one from the sanctuary this morning.

Well, if it isn't "Swear Word" Howard. Tell me, Howie, is this the only hour of the week when foul language doesn't come pouring out of that mouth of yours?

And here comes the cool clique. Every day I hear you call people names, humiliate them, and treat them like dirt simply because they're not "one of you." You'd better pray today that heaven has a special little section for you guys so you won't have to associate with these uncool people for all of eternity.

Brenda, Brenda, Brenda. You'd better get your eyes checked. I thought you were going to pop an optic nerve trying to see the answers to the chemistry quiz off of Quint's paper last Thursday.

JEREMIAH 10

Prepare to Build Thy God

OVERVIEW

The underlying problem causing the spiritual demise of the people of Judah was their readiness to forsake the true God and devote themselves to the worship of idols instead. So God challenges them—and us—to consider exactly what an idol is. Because the people of Judah will not turn from their idols, God repeats His plans to send invading forces from the north who will thoroughly defeat them.

OPENING ACT

Hand out copies of the reproducible sheet, "Choose God." This sheet introduces the issue of how people tend to perceive God. While your group members may not have carved stone idols in their homes, some of them may have "carved" *mental* images of what God is like. If so, they should reconsider those images during this session. The commandment not to make idols was intended to prevent people from perceiving God in limited ways. No portrait, statue, or other piece of art can come close to capturing even a portion of God's nature, so we aren't even to try. However we tend to perceive God, He is actually much larger than our perceptions.

DATE I USED THIS SESSION _____ GROUP I USED IT WITH _____

NOTES FOR NEXT TIME _____

_____

_____

1. What would you think of your neighbors if you happened to see through their window that they were having a worship service around an ugly little wooden idol? Would you think the same thing about a friend who spent practically every spare minute working on and driving his car—even the time he could be spending in church and youth group? What would be the difference?

2. What are some other "idols" that "regular people" are devoted to today? (Money, TV, work, or anything else that diverts attention from God on a regular basis may be an idol.)

3. The people of Judah had gotten so heavily involved with idols that they even had "family times" to worship the "Queen of Heaven" (7:18). Some were even sacrificing their children to other gods (7:31). But what, exactly, was it that the people were devoting themselves to (10:1-3)? (An idol was nothing more than a hunk of wood from a tree that had to be carved and decorated by other humans.)

4. According to Jeremiah 10:4, 5, what can the real God do that idols cannot? (Sit up without having to be nailed down; speak; move; act in loving or devastating ways.)

5. When the facts are stated so clearly, it seems foolish to put faith in idols. How would you explain the popularity of idolatry—then and now? (Perhaps people tend to want to put their faith in things they can see rather than in an unseen God.)

6. Even though God remains unseen, we can tell that He exists. How would you try to prove the physical existence of God to someone who is skeptical? Compare group members' responses with Jeremiah's references to the trembling earth (10:10); creation (10:12, 16); and thunder, clouds, and lightning (10:13).

7. The consequences of idolatry are severe. For Judah, the results were invasion and capture by the Babylonians from the north (10:17-22). For people today who serve idols such as money, power, possessions, or anything else, what do you think they can expect? (Someday those "gods" will prove as ineffective as the wooden gods of Judah. Unless God is in control of a person's life, he or she will ultimately experience significant problems and frustrations, as well as an emotional and spiritual void that cannot be filled.)

8. **What was Jeremiah's response as all of these truths sank in** (10:23-25)? (He wanted God to "check him out" to make sure that he was not at fault as well.) **Do you ever pray for God to take a close look at you and "correct" you? Why or why not?** (Many of us know of enough sin in our lives that we don't yet want God to inspect us.)

9. **Do you agree that it is up to God to "direct" the steps of His people** (10:23)? **Explain. Describe a time when you were headed down a particular path, only to discover that God was trying to lead you somewhere else.**

10. **How can we identify idolatry in our lives before it becomes a problem? How can we help friends deal with problems that threaten to become idolatry issues?**

(Needed: An assortment of craft materials)

Place an assortment of craft materials—cloth, modeling clay, wood, and so forth—on a table in front of your group members. Ask: **Can you imagine using these materials to build an image that we could then worship, offer sacrifices to, and trust to take care of us?** (Of course not.) **Then why is it that we sometimes trust our money to get us out of jams, or spend our time trying to impress a cute member of the other sex rather than trying to serve God, or do anything else that could be construed as idolatrous?** Don't let group members leave, satisfied that because they don't have any wooden idols they are exempt from trouble. Challenge each person to meticulously search his or her attitudes and behavior to see if anything is being allowed to become an idol—and to deal with any conflicts of interest that are discovered. Close the session with your own version of Jeremiah's prayer to "Correct me, Lord." Then give group members an opportunity for silent confession and repentance.

Choose God

Excuse us, but we hear that you're someone who knows God. We need an eyewitness to identify what He's like. You're looking through one-way glass, so you can see these people, but they can't see you. All we need you to do is identify which of these figures is the God you know.

If none of these subjects fits your image completely, do any of them even remotely resemble what you think of as "God"? Which ones, and in what ways?

We have our own artist who can help you out. Give us as complete a description as you can for what your God looks like.

Finally, how else would you suggest that we get an accurate description of God? Please be as specific as possible.

JEREMIAH 12

Life Isn't Fair!

OVERVIEW

Even though Jeremiah has been receiving God's message that the nation of Judah is soon going to be brought to its knees by the Babylonians, he is struggling with the age-old question of why wicked people seem to prosper while faithful people suffer. Actually, Jeremiah is beginning to see things more from God's perspective and appears eager to hasten the judgment on the sinful people of his own nation. God makes it clear that the people's sins are not being overlooked. He has a definite plan to deal with the problem, and while He has not yet taken action, it won't be long before He does.

OPENING ACT

Begin the session with a debate. At issue is the topic "God is always fair." If group members feel strongly one way or another, let them choose whether to defend the statement or oppose it. Divide those who don't feel as strongly to make the sides approximately even. You should moderate the debate to ensure that both sides have the opportunity to make points and raise questions for the other team. The debate should raise several questions, including "If God is always completely fair, why do good people suffer while evil people do quite well?" Let group members struggle for a while with the questions they raise; then move into the session, where kids will have additional opportunities for discussion.

DATE I USED THIS SESSION _____ GROUP I USED IT WITH _____

NOTES FOR NEXT TIME _____

_____

_____

Reading

1-4

5-13

14-17

eye & for an eye is human nature, but not Gods.

1. If you had to name the one thing that you think is most unfair about trying to live a Christian life, what would it be? How strongly do you feel about that particular issue? Why?

2. Jeremiah's complaint in Jeremiah 12 is that wicked people seem to prosper while good people struggle (12:1). Do you ever feel that way? Without naming names, what are some specific examples that you feel are unjust?

3. How do you handle such feelings? Do you ever tend to blame God? Or, like Jeremiah, do you ever wish wicked and selfish people would be dragged off "like sheep to be butchered" (12:3)? Explain.

4. What do you think it means that some people have God "on their lips but far from their hearts" (12:2)? (Some people profess to be good Christians, but refuse to behave as such. They make a mockery of God; they mislead others as to what a godly lifestyle should be; and they frustrate sincere people who try hard to be faithful.)

5. How do you think people get to be so defiant? (Since God doesn't *immediately* confront everyone who sins, some people begin to believe that He "will not see . . . us" [12:4].) **When you notice this tendency in other people, what's one thing you should think about?** (*Anyone* is capable of becoming defiant if he or she doesn't yield to God. Confession and repentance may be more important than we realize.)

6. God didn't seem to mind Jeremiah's honest question, but Jeremiah might not have liked God's answer. Read Jeremiah 12:5. **What do you think God meant?** (A loose translation might be "You ain't seen nothin' yet." The wicked people would *eventually* suffer [12:7-13], but Jeremiah would first suffer at their hands.)

7. Jeremiah saw wicked people who appeared to be fooling God and prospering. **What was God's perspective on those people** (12:7-13)? (He saw ungrateful people, ruining every good thing He had tried to give them.) **When**

people today seem to have fooled God, what do you think He sees?

8. Do you think God was ready to give up on His people completely (12:14-17)? Explain. (God receives no pleasure in disciplining His people. He will allow them to be carried away from their land, but only for a time. He will see them through their exile, during which time they will learn to trust Him again. He will then see that they eventually return.)

9. Who do you think are worse: people who scoff at God and refuse to yield to Him at all or those who profess to believe in Him in order to receive His blessings, but then pursue their own interests instead of His? Explain.

10. What can you learn from Jeremiah the next time you see people who seem to be prospering when they don't deserve to? (We need to be assured that God is in control of every situation, no matter what it appears to look like.)

Hand out copies of the reproducible sheet, "Complaint Form." Have group members list every unfair situation they can think of. Encourage them to be as detailed as possible and get everything out in the open. Then challenge them to think of their lives as an action movie. Explain: **In every good movie, the hero runs into strong opposition and unfair situations before he or she gets to the end. But what makes the movie good is his or her ability to overcome the problems and persevere until the end.** Point out that we're not even close to the end of our "movies" yet, so we can expect some ongoing opposition. The things that group members listed on their sheets are certainly "plot twists" that must be dealt with. But if your kids remain faithful and keep struggling to succeed, God promises them a "happy ending" (in the best sense of the expression).

Complaint Form

Dear Living Person:

The Management would like to ensure that your stay here (on earth) is a pleasurable experience in every way possible. So if something is not to your complete satisfaction, we would like to know. Please feel free to tell us about anything—no matter how big or small—that you would like to see changed. And please don't limit your complaints. We want to know about *everything.* Your comments will be greatly appreciated.

What complaints, if any, do you have about your surroundings (home, city, country, world, etc.)? *School, church*

What complaints, if any, do you have about the *people* with whom you must share your home, school, city, and so forth?

Do you have any comments to make about your personal "package" of strengths, weaknesses, emotions, thoughts, hopes, dreams, and so forth?

✳What could be provided for you that would make you more comfortable? (No expense is too great for you.)

JEREMIAH 13; 18; 24

As Plain as the Figs in Your Face

Much of the Book of Jeremiah to this point has been quite clear in detailing what God plans to do to the sinful and unrepentant nation of Judah. Yet sometimes an object lesson is an effective teaching tool, so God uses several different symbols to demonstrate what's going to happen to Judah—and why.

Hand out copies of the reproducible sheet, "Trick-Tac-Toe." Give group members a few minutes to try to figure out what the three pictures in each line (horizontally, vertically, and diagonally) have in common. The answers are as follows: *Vertical columns:* (1) kings; (2) caps; (3) beards; *Horizontal rows:* (1) pairs of people; (2) clubs; (3) teeth; *Diagonal lines:* (1) tea/tee/T; (2) balls. Afterward, explain that group members are about to discover what belts, wineskins, potters' wheels, and figs all have in common.

DATE I USED THIS SESSION _____ GROUP I USED IT WITH _____

NOTES FOR NEXT TIME _____

_____

_____

1. How many euphemisms or slang expressions can you think of to say that someone died or was killed? (Bought the farm; croaked; went to be with the Lord; etc.)

2. Why do you think God used parables and symbolic language to make points rather than simply saying what He meant? (God did make clear and plain statements, but He also used symbols. Different people respond to various things, so God uses assorted methods of communication.)

3. God used an object lesson to teach Jeremiah a lesson (13:1-11). What was the object and the lesson Jeremiah was supposed to learn? (A linen belt was hidden and then recovered several days later. But the belt, which had been good and useful, was so deteriorated that it was no longer good for anything. The belt was symbolic of the uselessness of God's people.)

4. What was the underlying problem of the people of Judah (13:9)? (Pride.) How can pride be just as dangerous to Christians today?

5. A belt that's too rotten to wear around your waist is no good. With what similar image did God follow that example (13:12-14)? (Wineskins that didn't contain what they were supposed to.) What was the point? (Just as good wine could be used purely for the purposes of getting drunk, God's people, who were intended for good, could turn bad and perform only negative actions.)

6. Another object lesson was witnessed by Jeremiah at the potter's house (18:1-12). The potter was at work, but when the pot didn't turn out right, he started over and reshaped the clay into a usable pot. What do you think God was trying to show Jeremiah? (When people rebel against God, He isn't "stuck" with them. He has the power to easily reshape them into what He knows they ought to be.)

7. Do you think the potter *wanted* to start over again when his first pot didn't turn out right? (No. But he would do whatever was necessary to see that the job was done right.) What does this object lesson tell us about God (18:11, 12)?

(God would like to see His people turn voluntarily from their evil ways. But if they don't, He will deal with them.)

8. **Even after the overthrow of Judah, Jeremiah's job was not finished. He spoke for God even *during* the people's captivity. And one of the first visions he had at that time was of two baskets of figs (24:1-10). What was God's point with this vision?** (Even in exile, God would look after His people. He already had plans to return them to their land with a new heart and a fresh relationship with Him.) **Does this mean God was giving His people "a slap on the wrist," after which everyone was going to be OK? Explain.** (God knew that some people still rejected Him, and He would have nothing else to do with them.)

9. **Of the people you know, what percentage would you say are "good figs" whom you expect to live their lives for God? What percentage would you put in the "bad fig" category, for which there is little hope?** (Thankfully, not all are predictable—remember the pre-church Paul.)

10. **Not only were the people rejecting God during this time, they rejected His messenger as well (18:18). Do you ever get harassed when you speak up for God? If so, in what ways?**

If your kids are starting to get the hang of symbolic imagery, give them an opportunity to create some symbols of their own. Let each person make a comparison for either good people or bad people. ("God's people are like _____ because _____." "Sinful people are like _____ because _____.") Your kids may not relate to linen belts, potters' wheels, wineskins, or figs, so let them come up with symbols that make sense to them. Then, to close the session, have kids give thanks for the best symbol of all: Jesus. He is the bread of life, the living water, the door, the way to God, and the perfect demonstration of God's nature. The study of Old Testament prophecy and doom should make us more thankful for the forgiveness we have for our sins and for our ready access to God at any time.

TRICK-TAC-TOE

On the tic-tac-toe diagram below, the set of pictures in each row, column, and diagonal line contains something in common. See how long it takes you to find all eight common bonds—one for each trio of pictures.

If You Buy It, They Will Come—Back

After repeated warnings by Jeremiah of impending invasion, the people of Judah are faced with the fact that the Babylonians are "at the door," so to speak—besieging Jerusalem. God tells Jeremiah to buy a field and put away the deed for a while. Even though God was allowing bad times to occur at this moment, He could see beyond them to when He would restore the land to His people. The Lord wanted Jeremiah to be just as confident that troublesome times would be followed by lasting periods of peace and rejoicing.

The reproducible sheet, "Panic Quiz," will help kids express how they handle times of stress and trouble. After a few minutes, ask volunteers to share their responses. Also ask them to describe the situations in which they feel most panicky. Point out that everyone experiences periods of panic from time to time; but if the same situations continually trigger such feelings, perhaps a closer evaluation can provide some reasons. Once the reasons are discovered, people can come up with options to help them deal with those feelings and learn to live without so much fear and panic in their lives.

DATE I USED THIS SESSION _____ GROUP I USED IT WITH _____

NOTES FOR NEXT TIME_____

_____

_____

1. When was the last time you felt extremely panicky about something? Was this a onetime panic attack, or is it a recurring problem? How do you respond when panic threatens to incapacitate you? Do you have any "tricks" to remain calm?

2. If you think *you* have problems, look at Jeremiah. The Babylonian army was attacking Judah, and the king of Judah had arrested Jeremiah for prophesying that the Babylonians would win (32:1-5). On a scale of one to ten, how much panic do you think you might feel under such conditions? Explain.

3. God gave Jeremiah a very strange command during this time. What was the prophet supposed to do (32:6-12)? (Buy a field.) Why in the world would Jeremiah want to buy land that would soon be claimed by one of the strongest empires ever to exist (32:15)? (Because God saw past the capture of His people to their return to the land. Jeremiah's purchase was an act of faith.)

4. Jeremiah's purchase was accompanied with a prayer of praise (32:16-25). When you're under a lot of pressure, do you ever stop to praise God for the *good* things you can think of, and to remember that He is still in charge? What "memory joggers" might you use to remember to do this more often?

5. Do you think there was any doubt that God was in charge of everything that was happening (32:26-29)? Explain. (God revealed to Jeremiah exactly what would happen, and it all came true.) Do you ever doubt—or perhaps wonder just a little bit—whether God is in complete control of what's going on in *your* life? If so, when? Why?

6. Do you think an invasion of the vicious Babylonians was really necessary to get the people of Judah's attention (32:30-35)? Explain. (The people weren't just a little bit sinful. They had completely abandoned God, choosing instead to worship other gods and participate in numerous detestable practices.) Do you ever think God is too harsh toward you—or your friends or family? Explain.

7. After the people suffer at the hands of the Babylonians and then turn back to God, what is in store for them (32:36-41)? (The same promises that would have been theirs if they had obeyed God to begin with—unity, peace, safety, and so forth.)

8. If God knew He was going to give all of these good things to His people in a few years anyway, why do you think the people had to go through such terrible times until then? (Some of the rebellious people needed to be weeded out during this time. Also, sin must be dealt with before forgiveness and restoration is possible. Hard times act as a purifying process for people honestly seeking to be faithful to God.)

9. Jeremiah had remained faithful to God all of this time. Why do you think he had to go through the captivity and exile with everyone else? (God's servants must serve where God's people are. If people were instantly rewarded for everything good they did, no one would be working with the people who need them.)

10. Does any particular area of your life seem like a "calamity" or a "desolate waste" right now (32:42-44)? (Perhaps family relationships, the future, dating relationships, etc.) **Do you believe the situation can possibly get better, or have you given up? What would it take for you to believe that God could restore hope in your life?**

Jeremiah bought a field during a war he knew his people would lose—now that's an act of faith. Challenge your group members to think of a similar act of faith to show that they trust God to take care of them—no matter what. If group members truly believe God will take care of *them*, perhaps they would be willing to help take care of others—by "adopting" a child in a foreign country, by taking a collection for missionaries, by helping the homeless in their neighborhoods, or whatever. Encourage kids to believe that God will see them through their own hard times and can help them set good examples for others along the way.

Panic Quiz

We all face crises from time to time. When you do, are you one of those people who remains cool, calm, and collected? Or are you scared, screaming, and discombobulated? Take the following test to see.

1. You walk into first period math class. The teacher says, "Get out your pencils. Today's the day for the quiz that will count for half of your grade." Unfortunately, you forgot about the quiz all weekend when you should have been studying. What do you do?

    (a) Run from the room, screaming something about having malaria.
    (b) Wait for the test to see if it's as hard as you suppose. If it is, you fake a heart attack.
    (c) Take the test, later explain to the teacher that you forgot to study, and plead for a make-up exam.
    (d) Other _____

2. While dog-sitting at a neighbor's house, you invite a date over. The two of you get involved in staring into each other's eyes. An hour later, you remember to check on the dog—and he's nowhere to be found. What do you do?

    (a) Call *America's Most Wanted* to turn yourself in.
    (b) Run through the neighborhood screaming the dog's name.
    (c) Conclude that unless it had a key, the dog couldn't have gotten outside. So you search the house until you find him.
    (d) Other _____

3. You're on a date—a first date with someone you've had your eyes on for a long time. You're in a very nice restaurant, but before the appetizer even arrives, you spill a large glass of water into your lap. The other person doesn't notice. What do you do?

    (a) Thump your forehead on the table and start pounding your fists against the table top, repeating "I'm such a loser" at the top of your lungs.
    (b) Sit there through the whole meal, and afterward keep saying, "I'm having so much fun, let's just sit here for a while longer" until you dry off.
    (c) Admit what happened and ask if you can run home to change.
    (d) Other _____

4. You're in the supermarket when a whole pyramid of canned corn crashes down in front of you. You didn't touch it. What do you do?

    (a) Do one of those *I Love Lucy* routines in which you try to get it all stacked back up before anyone notices.
    (b) Quickly move to the next aisle while you pin the blame on the nearest small child.
    (c) Go to the service desk and politely ask for a "clean up on Aisle 7."
    (d) Other _____

Maybe our situations don't press your panic buttons. If not, what are some situations in which you might really panic? How do you handle such panic attacks?

JEREMIAH 38

Pit Stop

Jeremiah's prophecies of Babylonian aggression begin to come true. His advice is to not fight the Babylonians, but to realize it is God's will for the people of Judah to be conquered. Consequently, he is perceived as a traitor. The people get upset and throw Jeremiah into a cistern with mud in the bottom. But Jeremiah has a friend who appeals to the king on his behalf, and he is rescued. Still, Jeremiah speaks the truth. His words are eventually borne out as Jerusalem is captured.

Have kids think of a recent situation that has been "the pits" for them—a time when they were depressed, dejected, despondent, or otherwise deeply upset. Then ask each person to act out the situation, using charades only—no talking. In most cases, the situation is likely to involve more than one person, so the person must think of a way to play all of the parts. Each person should act out his or her situation until the others guess what it is. Afterward, hand out copies of the reproducible sheet, "Well, Well, Well." Group members should consider *all* of the bad things in their lives and determine an appropriate "depth" to indicate how strongly they feel about each thing. When they're finished, let each person describe any "deep" problems that haven't already been mentioned. Use the activity to introduce Jeremiah's "pit" experience.

DATE I USED THIS SESSION _____ GROUP I USED IT WITH _____

NOTES FOR NEXT TIME _____

_____

_____

1. Have you ever felt like God had deserted you? If so, what were the circumstances? What did you do? How did the situation turn out?

2. When you suffer, do you believe that all you need to do is start obeying God to make everything all right again? Why or why not?

3. Jeremiah had done everything God wanted him to do. He had warned the people of Judah—repeatedly—that God was going to allow them to be captured by their enemies if they didn't repent. It all came true. But when the Babylonians showed up, what happened to Jeremiah (38:1-6)? (He was accused of siding with the enemy and thrown into a muddy cistern.)

4. As Jeremiah sank in the mud at the bottom of the well, how do you think he felt about the people who put him there? How do you think he felt about God? How do you think he felt about himself? (We can't be sure, but he must have seen that his faithfulness to God did not result in immediate gratification.)

5. So God's faithful prophet sinks in mud at the bottom of a well where he could be killed by angry people at any minute, or eventually starve to death. Of all of the miraculous ways God could have rescued him, what do you think happened (38:7-13)? (A friend appealed to the king on Jeremiah's behalf, and the king had Jeremiah pulled up. God frequently chooses to work through friends, family members, and means that may not seem impressive, but are just as effective as miracles.)

6. Do you think the king didn't believe Jeremiah or just didn't *want* to believe him? Explain. See if your group members can think of times when they ignored someone's good advice just because they didn't like the person for some reason.

7. King Zedekiah didn't want to deal with Jeremiah publicly, but he set up a private meeting for advice (38:14-23). What problems were on his mind? (Battle strategy, concern for the lives of himself and his family, treachery by those who had already deserted to the Babylonian side, the future of the city of Jerusalem, etc.)

8. **When someone mistreats you, do you automatically take it personally? Do you ever stop to consider that the person might be under tremendous pressure and is taking it out on you because you happen to be around? Explain.**

9. **The meeting between Zedekiah and Jeremiah proved that the king *did* need the prophet. But the king didn't want anyone else to know that, and begged Jeremiah to keep their conversation a secret** (38:24-28). **How would you have felt in Jeremiah's place? What would you have done?** (It must have been a temptation to yell, "Look, everybody, the king *does* believe in me!")

10. **When you suffer even after you've been faithful to God, how do you feel? Are you convinced God will reward you someday? Or is your tendency ever to give up and join the rest of the crowd who do whatever they want to do and don't seem to suffer for it?** Emphasize that God certainly rewards faithfulness. But occasional suffering is "par for the course" for any Christian. One's degree of suffering is not always a valid indicator of God's closeness or distance.

Some people say, "When life gives you lemons, make lemonade." On a similar level, see if your group members are up to the challenge of "When life puts you in the pits, have fun in the mud." Plan a Mud Fest. Find a place that you can hose down where you can play tug-of-war, football, volleyball, or any other grimy, filthy, messy activity you can think of. Determine a time, wear your oldest clothes (and bring an extra set), and see exactly how much fun you can have. While we may try to avoid getting dirty in our spiritual lives, sometimes we're going to be "stuck in the mud." Help group members see that it's not always such a terrible thing.

Well, Well, Well

People sometimes speak of being "down," "in the pits," "in the dumps," "lower than a snake's belly," "at rock bottom," . . . well, you get the idea. The problem is that we don't always explain exactly *how far* down we're feeling. That's what this well is for. Think of every rotten, lousy, horrible, traumatic, unpleasant thing that has happened to you recently. Then, for each thing, write it in at the appropriate "depth" in this bottomless well.

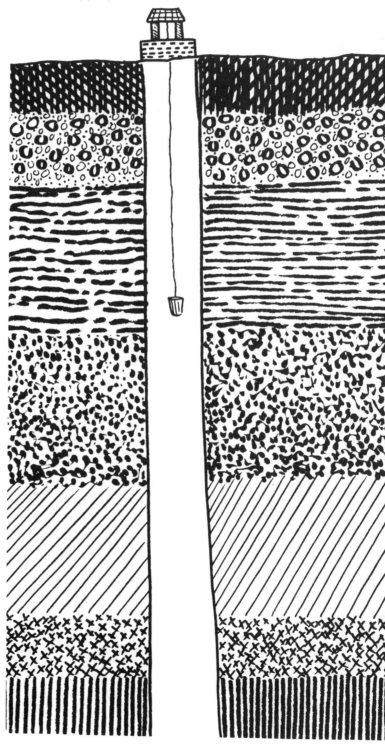

Six feet under

Way down deep

Can't even see the light at the top

Deeper than anyone can accurately describe

LAMENTATIONS

Jere's Lament

The Babylonian invasion of Judah and the subsequent capture of the city of Jerusalem is one of the darkest periods in Old Testament history. Everything the prophets had warned about comes to pass. With the invasion come horrible conditions. Slaughter is everywhere. Starving mothers are driven to cannibalism of their own children to survive. All of the blessings God had provided for His people—especially their relationship with Him and worship privileges—are gone. The nation is split, with the best of the people carried off into captivity. Yet Jeremiah is able to look past all of this to see God at work. Jeremiah can praise God, even now, for His great faithfulness.

As group members assemble, hand out paper and pencils. Explain that you're going to have a "sad writing contest." Ask group members to write a story, song, or poem that they feel will certainly make everyone sad. The work should take no longer than thirty seconds to read. After a designated time, let group members read what they've written. Designate a winner. Then explain that few works of fiction or contrived plots are ever as tragic as some of the actual things that happen to people we love. Such was the case in Judah during Jeremiah's writing of Lamentations.

DATE I USED THIS SESSION _____ GROUP I USED IT WITH _____

NOTES FOR NEXT TIME _____

_____

_____

1. **What do you think is absolutely the worst thing that could happen to a person?** (Dying may be the first thing to come to mind. Yet life after abuse, a rape, an accident that leaves a person blind or crippled, or something serious that happens to a loved one might seem worse.)

2. Read Lamentations 1:1-11. Point out that it is written in a poetic style. Then ask: **How do you think Jeremiah's sad writing compares to yours?**

3. **Of all of the problems Jeremiah lists in the first eleven verses of Lamentations, what do you think is the worst? Explain.** (Perhaps the fact that the people brought these catastrophes upon themselves [1:8, 9].)

4. **It's clear that God's people had become very sinful and had forsaken Him. But why do you think God allowed people who were even more wicked to defeat them?** (God had a purpose in all of this tragedy. He was doing what was necessary to turn His people around so they could receive all of the things He wanted them to have. And He uses whatever means necessary to accomplish His purposes.)

5. **There's no doubt that God was behind the Babylonian invasion** (2:17). **The image Jeremiah uses is one of God temporarily becoming the enemy of Judah** (2:1-5). **Do you ever feel as if God is** *your* **enemy? Explain.**

6. **Do you think God was literally an enemy of His people? Explain.** (God protects us from much that can harm us. So if He withdraws His hand for a time [2:3], we might feel as if He is against us. God opposes sin, not His people. If we eliminate the sin from our lives, we need never feel that God is against us.)

7. **When God's protection was removed from Judah, exactly how bad did things get for the people** (4:6-10; 5:10-15)? (The people faced cannibalism, rape, intense hunger, and more.) **The people of Judah had once known God's full blessing. How might that have made the terrible things that were now happening even worse?** (The contrast must have been devastating.)

8. Jeremiah had advance notice that this tragedy was coming. How do you suppose he felt when it finally arrived? (Jeremiah was perhaps the one person able to see past what was happening to a time when God would restore His good relationship with the people.)

9. Read Lamentations 3:22-33. Why do you think these verses are right in the middle of the Book of Lamentations? Do you think they belong there? Explain.

10. Could you have witnessed everything that was going on, and still managed to think about the great faithfulness and everlasting compassion of God? Do you think Jeremiah was special in some way? What would need to change before *you* could see past all of the bad things in life to see mostly good things again?

Continue your discussion of the last question as you hand out sheets of paper and pencils. Have group members list every problem they are currently facing—no matter how large or small. Then hand out copies of the reproducible sheet, "Sleep on It." Challenge group members to be honest about the negative events of life and the pain produced by them. Let kids work individually on their sheets at first, trying to recall promising things that will encourage them. Then work as a group, asking individuals to share the things they came up with for Steps 3 and 4. Many of the promises and observations of one person may be just as applicable for others. Afterward, encourage group members to use their sheets for at least a week—to begin each day by reviewing the compassion and faithfulness of God. Have them report at your next meeting to see if such reminders make a difference in the way they deal with the troublesome events of their lives.

Sleep on It

"Because of the Lord's great love we are not consumed, for His compassions never fail. They are new every morning; great is your faithfulness"

(Lamentations 3:22, 23).

Some people seem to think that leading a successful Christian life means ignoring everything negative. But sometimes bad things come into our lives for a purpose. After all, if we never faced any unpleasant circumstances or bad news, how could we truly know that God is powerful enough to see us through our problems? Your relationship with God should be able to sustain you through any negative circumstances you will ever face. If you don't believe it, try the following plan of action.

Step # 1: *List every bad thing that's happening in your life right this minute.*
Don't be afraid to admit that bad stuff happens to you. Be specific. Think of everything that's unfair, painful, frustrating, and otherwise unpleasant.

Step # 2: *Before you go to bed each night, talk to God about your list.*
Tell Him exactly what's happening, why it hurts, and why you don't think it's fair. (God's pretty big—He can take it.) If you're not honest with Him, He can't help you with your situation.

Step # 3: *List all of the biblical promises you can think of that apply to your situation.*
If you can't think of any, you probably haven't been doing enough Bible reading lately. There are all sorts of promises about power, comfort, companionship, peace, and other things you need when bad times come. If you still need help, consult a Bible concordance or some of your Christian friends or church leaders.

Step # 4: *The moment you wake up, begin to thank God for everything you can think of.*
Start with the fact that you woke up to experience another day of life, with all of its surprises. Start your list before you do anything else. Shake the groggy feeling out of your brain and start looking around you. As you get better at this, you should keep finding new things you didn't think of the day before.

Step # 5: *Repeat the cycle every day.*
Keep listing your undesired circumstances. Keep talking to God. Keep thinking of biblical promises. Keep looking for new instances of God's power, compassion, faithfulness, and so forth. Before long, you should notice something: even though bad things keep happening, you see them differently. They're not so . . . bad any more. Well, they're still bad, but you should discover an amazing new ability to cope with them that you never knew was possible.

EZEKIEL 1

Ain't Nothing Like the Wheel Things

As Ezekiel is called by God to become a prophet, he is shown a vision. The vision includes creatures with four faces, wings, and intersecting wheels by which they appear to move. Above these creatures is a throne. On the throne is another figure that has the appearance of a man—a man that looks like glowing metal, full of fire and surrounded by brilliant light. All Ezekiel can do in the presence of the Lord is fall on his face.

Begin the session by playing some of your kids' favorite games. But prearrange with one volunteer to come late—just as you're beginning the "real" part of the session. Have your latecomer announce that he or she has just had an encounter with a UFO. This person's description of the UFO should be very similar to Ezekiel's account of the creatures in Ezekiel 1. The rest of the kids are certain to be skeptical. Let them ask questions, with the volunteer answering them as well as he or she can. After a few minutes, ask group members why they didn't believe the story. Then, as you move into your study of Ezekiel 1, help kids see what a problem Ezekiel might have had in being taken seriously after reporting his vision.

DATE I USED THIS SESSION _____ GROUP I USED IT WITH _____

NOTES FOR NEXT TIME _____

_____

_____

1. If God appeared before you in a majestic vision, and if He didn't tell you to keep His appearance a secret, who would you tell about your experience? Why? (Perhaps some of your group members would try to get on "Donahue" or "Oprah" to tell the world about it. Others might tell only close friends and family members. Others might keep the experience to themselves.)

2. What do you think life would be like in God's presence? How does it make you feel to realize that there are many things going on that we can't see and that we don't know about?

3. God occasionally gives people a "peek" at what life is like in the spiritual realm (Isaiah 6; Jeremiah 1; II Corinthians 12:1-4; Revelation 21–22). Why do you think He doesn't just have a heavenly "open house" one day to show everyone? (It takes maturity and responsibility to live with such knowledge. Many people might find the sights too frightening, too bizarre, or too overwhelming.)

4. Ezekiel got to see the glory of God—as well as some of God's angelic attendants. Read Ezekiel 1:4-14. When you think of angels, is this the image that usually comes to mind? If not, how do you picture them? What would you do if you suddenly found yourself surrounded by these beings? Explain.

5. The creatures had wings, and they could fly. But they also had an unusual form of ground transportation. How did they maneuver (1:15-21)? (They had some kind of "intersecting wheels" that allowed them to move any direction while facing ahead.) How does this compare to most of the futuristic, science-fiction beings you've seen portrayed? (Movement of fictional futuristic characters is usually portrayed as being clumsy and labored. The creatures Ezekiel saw seem to move smoothly and effortlessly—"like flashes of lightning" [1:14].)

6. In addition to what Ezekiel was seeing, what was he hearing? See Ezekiel 1:22-24. A natural tendency might be to think, *I'm seeing things,* or *I'm dreaming.* Do you think

Ezekiel had any doubts as to what he was seeing? Explain.

7. Ezekiel's attention is drawn from the creatures to the throne of God Himself (1:25-28). How does your image of God compare with Ezekiel's description?

8. If you suddenly realized that you were in the actual presence of God, what would you immediately do? What emotions would you feel? Explain.

9. Would you like to have an experience like Ezekiel's? Why or why not?

10. When people eventually get to heaven, do you think the scene will be much as Ezekiel described? Or do you think things will be a bit more "casual"? Explain. (It may be similar, but we will have the benefit of not being there in our earthly, imperfect bodies [I Corinthians 15:35-58].)

11. If you were in God's presence, and if He gave you the opportunity to ask Him any question, what would you ask? Why?

Point out that Ezekiel was already a priest when God appeared to him, but that his visions surely improved his understanding of who God is. Most people can benefit by thinking more deeply about God's nature and His will. Because God remains unseen most of the time, it is rather easy to take lightly His commands and His leading. Yet if we were to get one glimpse of the God that Ezekiel saw, we might respond very differently. The reproducible sheet, "A Different Perspective," challenges group members to reconsider some of the behaviors and decisions they may have been taking a bit too lightly until now. Help kids see that their perceptions of God can make a major difference in how they respond to Him. Encourage them to read the first chapter of Ezekiel every day during the following week, followed by a period of prayer to the God described there. While we can certainly be thankful for God's grace, mercy, forgiveness, and friendship, we should never overlook His power and His glory.

Be honest. If these were two of your teachers, do you think you'd treat them with the same level of respect? Why or why not?

The perceptions we have about people help determine how we respond to them. If we know there's nothing they can do to hurt us, we might tend to do whatever we want to do when we're around them. But if *we* have a certain level of "fear" and/or respect for them, we may do whatever they tell us to do.

The same is true about God. If we perceive Him as only a "good buddy" or a casual acquaintance, we might have one response when He wants us to do something. But if we see Him in His full majesty (as Ezekiel did), we might have quite a different response. For each of the following situations, predict what your response would be in both cases.

A DiFFERENT PERSPECTIVE

	Response If I Have Only a Casual Knowledge of God	Response If I Have a Clear Understanding of God
You know you should go to church and Sunday school every week, but Sunday morning is prime sleeping time.		
At work, you're expected to look the other way when fellow employees "borrow" money from the cash register.		
A kid at school makes fun of your Christian beliefs, but you could easily beat up the little weasel.		
Your parents want you home earlier on weeknights. You don't think they'll really do anything serious if you ignore them, though.		
While spending the weekend with a friend, you and several friends figure it's a good time to see what it's like to get drunk. Your host's parents are out of town, and no one is going to drive home. Nobody will ever find out.		

What are some situations you're currently facing in which your perception of God might make a major difference in a decision or behavior?

EZEKIEL 2–3

Making a Prophet

Ezekiel's magnificent vision of God and His cherubim continues in Ezekiel 2–3 as God calls Ezekiel to be a prophet. Ezekiel is instructed to live among "rebellious" people, who may or may not listen to him. But God makes it clear that Ezekiel isn't responsible for the people's response; he is only responsible for his own faithfulness in speaking what God gives him to say.

(Needed: Blindfolds, game supplies)

Have kids form teams. Select one person from each team to stand at one end of the room. Everyone else should be blindfolded at the other end of the room. After the kids are blindfolded, set up an obstacle course, using pieces of paper on the floor labeled "Waterfall," "Cliffs," "Wild Animals," etc. (You might also use piles of blocks that will make noise if they're knocked over.) Explain that the goal is for each "seeing" person to shout instructions to his or her team members to direct them through the obstacle course. If a player touches one of the obstacles, he or she is out. The team that gets the most members safely across wins. Afterward, explain that your "seeing" members have been acting as watchmen or prophets. This will be further explained during the session.

DATE I USED THIS SESSION _____ GROUP I USED IT WITH _____

NOTES FOR NEXT TIME _____

_____

_____

1. Have you ever been responsible for the well-being of other people? If so, what were the circumstances? (Perhaps as a baby-sitter or a lifeguard.) **How did you feel about your responsibility? Why?** Point out that the job of a prophet involved overseeing people's spiritual well-being.

2. Most of us know, generally, what God expects of us because it's spelled out in the Bible. But if you suddenly found yourself standing in front of God with no one else around, and He *verbally* told you to do the same things, do you think it would make a difference in how you responded? Explain.

3. It might seem thrilling to get instructions directly from God. But do you think anything might keep you from being *completely* thrilled in such a situation? See Ezekiel 2:1-4. (The emotions might depend on the instructions being received. Ezekiel's job for God was not going to make him very popular.)

4. How would you feel if God personally selected you for a special mission, but you couldn't convince anyone to do what God said to do (2:5-7)? (Many people might feel like failures under such circumstances. But Ezekiel's responsibility was only to speak the truth—not to force people to change. God knew the people wouldn't listen to His prophet.)

5. People today sign contracts or shake hands to seal a deal. What did God have Ezekiel do instead? See Ezekiel 2:8–3:3. **Later we see that Ezekiel's message to the people was one of judgment and misery. So why do you think the scroll tasted sweet?** (God's Word is always fair. God is the source of sweetness. The sins of God's people, on the other hand, are a source of bitterness.)

6. Read Ezekiel 3:4-9. **Why might it be appropriate to pray that God would make us "hard heads"?** (If we become less sensitive to the comments of ungodly people, we might be more willing to speak up for God more regularly.)

7. Jeremiah had been a prophet *before* his nation went into captivity. Ezekiel was being sent to speak to the people after they had already been carried away from their country. **Which prophet's job do you think would be harder? Why?** (Jeremiah suffered because he dared prophesy the fall of his country. But both prophets tried to convince the people that God was really behind the events that were taking place.)

8. As Ezekiel left God's presence, he seems to have adopted God's emotions toward the people (3:12-15). He was too overwhelmed to speak for seven days. Later God explained that the job of a prophet was much like that of a watchman (3:16-21). **In what ways?** (A watchman's job was to sound the alarm when he saw trouble approaching. He wasn't held responsible for whether or not people heeded his call. The same was true of God's prophets.)

9. God imposed limitations on Ezekiel's contact with the people—both physically and verbally (3:22-27). **How do you think your life would change if you spoke only when God gave you something significant to say?**

10. If you had the opportunity to actually see and hear God, but then had to assume the responsibility given to Ezekiel, **would you do it? Why or why not? Would you want to ask questions first or have anything clarified? If so, what? How would you feel?**

The reproducible sheet, "E. Zeke Keel: Kid Prophet," challenges group members to think in terms of having a God-sent prophet in their midst—in a number of familiar settings. Give kids a few minutes to complete the sheet. When they're finished, let volunteers share some of the captions they came up with. Then say: **Many people think God doesn't send prophets anymore. Couldn't your school use one if there's so much sinful stuff going on?** If no one mentions it, point out that Christians are supposed to be the ones to set good examples and speak up for what is right. Close the session with a challenge for each person to do one "prophetic" thing this week—to make a statement for God whether or not anyone listens.

E. Zeke Keel: Kid Prophet

Have you heard? Prophets aren't just for adults any more! Meet Zeke. He's been sent to your school to let you know what God thinks about some of the things that are going on. In each of the settings below, fill in what you think he might say. (By the way, in addition to being a prophet, Zeke is pretty clever. So don't have him saying anything boring. OK?)

EZEKIEL 18

The Sins of the Fathers

During their exile, the people of Israel quote a proverb that places the blame for the demise of their nation on their parents and former generations. But God, through Ezekiel, makes it perfectly clear that each person is responsible for his or her own sins.

Have kids form teams. Give each team pencils and paper. Call one person from each team to read one of the following proverbs. At your signal, those people should begin to draw the proverb for their team members until one team correctly guesses what it is. Here are some proverbs you may use:
• The squeaky wheel gets the grease.
• A stitch in time saves nine.
• All work and no play makes Jack a dull boy.
• There's no time like the present.

Conclude with the proverb from Ezekiel 18:2—"The fathers eat sour grapes, and the children's teeth are set on edge." Drawing and guessing this proverb should provide a provocative introduction to the session.

DATE I USED THIS SESSION _____ GROUP I USED IT WITH _____

NOTES FOR NEXT TIME_____

_____

_____

1. Have you ever been blamed for or suffered the consequences of something someone else did? If so, what were the circumstances? How did you feel?

2. Do you have any problems or bad habits that you tend to blame on your parents? If so, what are they? Why do you blame your parents?

3. The "sour grapes" proverb (18:1, 2) may have originated from the statement in the Ten Commandments that God is "a jealous God, punishing the children for the sin of the fathers to the third and fourth generation" (Exodus 20:5). Does that mean that if God gets angry at something your parents do, He'll take it out on you? Explain. (Though the *consequences* of sin can pass to future generations, God does not punish people for things they haven't done.)

4. Read Ezekiel 18:5-9. God wanted to make sure that people didn't misunderstand His accountability system. Do you notice anything unusual or surprising about this description of Person #1? If no one mentions it, point out that God doesn't evaluate time spent in church, length of prayers, or other things that we might consider religious or spiritual. Rather, the integrity of the person and his or her relationships are what God notices.

5. Read Ezekiel 18:10-13. In contrast, look at Person #2, the child of Person #1. You may not know any idol worshipers or flat-out adulterers, but can you make similar comparisons using characteristics you witness in people at school? What behaviors do you think God notices and rewards? What behaviors does He despise?

6. Do you know of cases like this one, in which a good parent has a child that turns out to be completely rotten? If it's not the parents' fault, why do you think some kids turn out so different from their parents?

7. Read Ezekiel 18:14-18. Is God going to hold Person #3 responsible because his father was a creep? Explain. What can we learn from this example? (When we see weaknesses in our parents, we don't have to adopt those particular traits or habits. We can choose to be more obedient to God in those areas.)

8. How does it feel to know that your spiritual status is up to you—that you have no one to blame but yourself if your spiritual life isn't everything you want it to be?

9. Some people felt that God was being unfair when He took away their "excuse" for not being the people they ought to be (18:25-32). **What excuses do people today use for being less devoted to God than they should be?** (Lack of time, difficulty in understanding the Bible, the fact that God cannot be seen, etc.) **What do you think is the real reason for their failure to obey?** (Usually the problem is lack of sufficient effort.)

10. What are some things you might be able to do *with your family* so that both your generation and the previous one can grow closer to God at the same time?

Hand out copies of the reproducible sheet, "More or Less." Ask group members to fill out the chart as instructed. After a few minutes, say: **Suppose a tragedy occurs this week in which both of your parents are killed. You continue to live on your own and go about life pretty much the same way as before. But now you get to make all of the decisions for what should be done. Knowing that you have this kind of freedom and responsibility, go back through the sheet and mark where you think you would be in each area six months from now.** Have group members use a different kind of mark (perhaps a square instead of a circle) to differentiate their second group of responses from the first. Afterward, ask: **If your parents were suddenly taken out of the picture, do you think you would become more spiritual or less spiritual than you are right now? Why? What specific areas would need the most work? Why?** Close with a challenge for group members to stop relying so much on parents or making other excuses when it comes to spiritual commitment.

More
or LESS

When it comes to being the people God wants us to be, sometimes we're pretty good at it. Other times, however . . . well, let's just say we could use some work. So from time to time it's good to "take a reading"—to see how you're doing right this minute. In each of the following categories, circle the level where you feel you are at this point in your life. (Answers should be based on recent behavior, not on where you think you *should* be.) A "1" indicates little, if any, interest or participation in the activity. A "10" indicates that this is something to which you are continually devoted.

Attending church	1	2	3	4	5	6	7	8	9	10
Treating members of the opposite sex with total respect	1	2	3	4	5	6	7	8	9	10
Refusing to pick on other people	1	2	3	4	5	6	7	8	9	10
Repaying loans	1	2	3	4	5	6	7	8	9	10
Exercising complete honesty	1	2	3	4	5	6	7	8	9	10
Giving (money, clothes, unused items) to the needy	1	2	3	4	5	6	7	8	9	10
Lending money willingly to others—with no strings attached	1	2	3	4	5	6	7	8	9	10
Staying out of places you shouldn't go	1	2	3	4	5	6	7	8	9	10
Treating all people as equals—not showing favoritism	1	2	3	4	5	6	7	8	9	10
Obeying everything you know God wants you to do	1	2	3	4	5	6	7	8	9	10
Getting involved in youth group	1	2	3	4	5	6	7	8	9	10
Studying the Bible on your own	1	2	3	4	5	6	7	8	9	10
Praying on your own	1	2	3	4	5	6	7	8	9	10
Telling other people about Jesus	1	2	3	4	5	6	7	8	9	10

EZEKIEL 37

Re-animator

It might be hard for a nation of people who had been conquered and carried away by their enemies to hope that things could ever get better. But to prove that there is no limit to His power to restore life to a spiritually dry people, God demonstrates that He can even restore life to bones that had long ago dried out in the sun. Ezekiel witnesses the bones coming back together and once again being covered with flesh—but even then they remain dead. Only God's breath (Spirit) can provide the power they need to live. God also shows Ezekiel another sign to indicate that his scattered countrymen will eventually be reunited under a single king.

(Needed: Buckets of fried chicken or jigsaw puzzles)

Have kids form teams. Give each team a bucket of fried chicken. Have a contest to see which team can do the best job of reassembling the pieces to get a complete chicken. (In lieu of such a "grease fest," give teams a ridiculously short time to assemble a jigsaw puzzle.) Afterward, point out that things tend to come apart a lot easier than they go back together. Then explain that no matter how "apart" we may feel, God has the power to restore us to wholeness if we allow Him to do so. Use the activity to lead in to a discussion of Ezekiel 37.

DATE I USED THIS SESSION _____ GROUP I USED IT WITH _____

NOTES FOR NEXT TIME _____

_____

_____

1. Have you ever broken or damaged something and then tried to patch it up before anyone found out? If so, what were the circumstances? Did you get away with it? What happened?

2. Suppose I showed you a stack of old, dried-out bones, and asked if you thought they could ever come back to life. What would be your response? Why?

3. When God showed Ezekiel a pile of bones and asked him the same question, the prophet wasn't as skeptical as many of us would be. Ezekiel said, in effect, "They can live again if you say so" (37:1-3). **What do you think made Ezekiel so incredibly full of faith?** (He had already seen many awesome sights, including a vision of God's throne and His angels [Ezekiel 1]. His understanding of God's capabilities had grown a lot based on what he had seen.)

4. Why do you think God had *Ezekiel* speak to the bones (37:4-8)? **Why didn't God just work as Ezekiel watched?** (Just as Jesus later tried to encourage the disciples to get more involved in the miracles God was performing [Matthew 14:16], God chose to work through Ezekiel to demonstrate His power to the prophet.)

5. The bones went through a two-part "reunion." First, they came together and were covered with skin, but were still dead. Then when Ezekiel spoke to them a second time (37:9, 10), breath entered them and they came fully to life. **Do you think there was any purpose to this two-part process? If so, what was it?** (It seems to symbolize that we can be fully functioning, but not completely alive unless God's Spirit [37:14] is within us.)

6. God explained what this mysterious sight meant in regard to the people of Israel (37:11-14). **Can you think of any significance it might have for you or for people you know?** Encourage kids to give specific examples of people who might truly "come to life" if they would allow God to control them instead of trying to handle everything themselves.

7. God emphasized His message with yet another object lesson for Ezekiel (37:15-23). **Why do you think God gave the prophet another sign with the same meaning?** (Ezekiel was the only witness of the first sign—the united bones. The second sign—the united sticks—was intended for public display.)

8. **Why do you think the promise to be under one king again** (37:22-28) **was significant to God's people?** (It was a privilege that they'd once had—one that they took for granted. Now that they had lost it and were scattered to many different places, they could realize how special it was.)

9. **Have you ever lost something that you didn't appreciate until it was gone? Explain.**

10. **It seems that the moral of Ezekiel 37 is that no separation is too great for God to repair. If dry and bleached bones can be brought together into a living body again, any kind of reunion should be possible. Can you think of friends, family members, or others with whom you need to restore a relationship?** Let volunteers who are willing describe the relationships that come to mind. Explain that just because God can do the impossible doesn't mean we should put off making up until getting back together takes a literal miracle.

Explain that relationships aren't the only things that tend to drift apart. Our own actions, attitudes, and thoughts can begin to stray from what we know they ought to be. Therefore, we need to act before waiting too long. Hand out copies of the reproducible sheet, "Bone Dry." Let kids label any "loose bones" that may need to be reconnected to the skeleton. Remind kids that continued disobedience had eventually caused the people of Israel to experience failure, humiliation, captivity, exile in foreign countries, and other major losses. God was correcting the problem. But those losses wouldn't have been necessary if the people had only repented. Close the session with silent prayer, encouraging kids to confess anything they've recently been reluctant to talk to God about.

B O N E   D R Y

When God showed Ezekiel a pile of dry bones that were able to come back together and live again, He was demonstrating that nothing is ever "too far gone" for Him to repair. Perhaps you've felt yourself drifting away from God lately in one or more ways. If so, use the illustration below to identify which of your "bones" are causing problems. (For example, if you keep going places you shouldn't, perhaps your foot bone shouldn't be taking you there. Or if you drink things that are ille-gal or unwise, perhaps your "throat bone" shouldn't be so accommodating.)

Whatever the problem, mark all of the bones that need to be restored to good working condition. Beside each bone you mark, identify the specific problem and what you would like to see God help you do to get back in good working order.

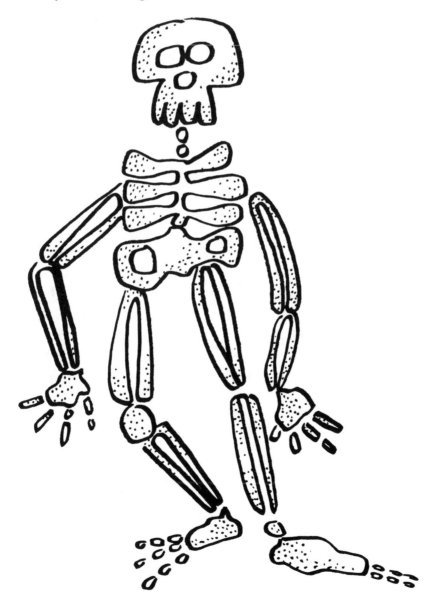

DANIEL 1

Eat Your Vegetables

After Judah is invaded by the Babylonians and the people are taken captive, King Nebuchadnezzar orders that the finest young male Israelites be trained for government service. Among those chosen are Daniel and three of his friends— Shadrach, Meshach, and Abednego. The four Israelites refuse to defile themselves by eating the king's food. Instead, they stay healthy by eating nothing but vegetables and water. Daniel and his friends later become trusted advisers to the king.

Hand out copies of the reproducible sheet, "The Book of Daniel: A Preview." Let kids work in pairs to complete the sheet. Announce that kids may use their Bibles during the quiz. To check kids' answers, use a "sword drill" approach. Read one of the questions on the sheet. The first team to stand and give you the correct answer gets a point. The team with the most points at the end of the game is the winner. (The correct answers are as follows: [1] a; [2] e; [3] a, b, c, d; [4] b; [5] e; [6] a; [7] c; [8] a; [9] e; [10] d; [11] b, c, d; [12] f; [13] g; [14] a; [15] e.) Afterward, briefly discuss what an interesting book Daniel is—full of action, intrigue, mysterious visions and dreams, and other things. Point out that questions 1, 3, 4, 6, 7, 10, and 15 come into play in this session.

DATE I USED THIS SESSION _____ GROUP I USED IT WITH _____

NOTES FOR NEXT TIME _____

_____

_____

1. If you knew that you were going to be forcibly taken from your home tomorrow to live in another country for several years, what three things would you want to take with you? Why?

2. Why did the Lord deliver Judah into the hands of the Babylonians (1:2)? (The people of Judah were idolatrous; the Lord was trying to teach them a lesson.)

3. Why do you think King Nebuchadnezzar wanted young Israelite men trained for service in his government (1:3, 4)? (Perhaps there was a shortage of qualified leaders in his country. Perhaps he thought that if he involved Israelite young men in his government, the rest of the captured Israelites would be less likely to rebel.)

4. Why do you think Nebuchadnezzar had Daniel and his friends renamed (1:6, 7)? (Perhaps he was trying to "erase" their Jewish identities—including their religious orientation—and give them Babylonian identities. "Daniel" means "God is my judge"; "Belteshazzar" means "Bel [a Babylonian god] protects his life.")

5. The royal food and wine probably included the finest delicacies in Babylon. So why was Daniel concerned about defiling himself by partaking of them (1:8)? (The first portion of the food and wine from the king's table was offered to idols. Also, the food was not prepared according to the regulations of Jewish law. Daniel was trying to maintain his Jewish identity and remain loyal to God's law.)

6. Daniel proposed a test to prove that God's sustenance—vegetables and water—was more nourishing than the finest foods in Babylon (1:8-14). What does Daniel's proposal tell us about him? (He was logical: rather than going on a "hunger strike for God," he proposed an experiment that could be measured visually. He had faith that God would sustain him. He was concerned for others—he recognized that if he and his friends began to look malnourished, the official in charge of training would be killed. He was persuasive.)

7. After ten days of eating nothing but vegetables and water, Daniel and his friends looked healthier than the men who ate the food from the king's table (1:15). **Is this a testimony to the benefits of a vegetarian diet? Explain.** (Certainly vegetables are a valuable asset in human diet, but Jewish law allowed other foods. Underlying all of this was God's provision in sustaining His obedient children.)

8. **Compare Daniel's situation in Daniel 1 with Joseph's situation in Genesis 39–41. What similarities do you see?** (Both young men were being held in a foreign country against their will. Both were protected by God in amazing ways. Both were able to interpret dreams. Both rose to high ranks in the foreign government and became trusted advisers to the king. Both refused to deny God in the midst of rampant idolatry.)

9. **What do you think was Daniel's primary motivation in life?** (To please and obey God; to be true to his identity as one of God's people.)

10. **What can you learn from this story that might apply to a situation in your life right now?**

Read I Peter 2:11. Ask: **In what ways are Christians in a position like Daniel's?** If no one mentions it, point out that we are "aliens" in this world just as Daniel was an alien in Babylon. We also face people in our society who want us to change our "identity"—to forget that we're Christians. Encourage group members to take a stand for their faith just as Daniel did. Ask them to think of something they might give up (like a sinful habit) or develop (like a more active testimony) to emphasize their identity as Christians. Close the session by having group members write letters to God, explaining what they're going to do and asking for His help as they attempt to stand up for Him.

The Book of Daniel: A PREVIEW

Match the following characters in the Book of Daniel with the correct descriptions. For some characters, more than one description may apply. Likewise, some descriptions may apply to more than one character. If you don't know an answer, make your best guess.

a. Daniel

b. Shadrach

c. Meshach

d. Abednego

e. King Nebuchadnezzar

f. King Belshazzar

g. King Darius

_____ 1. He was also known as Belteshazzar.

_____ 2. He dreamed of a large statue and an enormous tree.

_____ 3. He refused to eat the delicacies and drink the wine from the king's table, choosing instead to eat only vegetables and drink only water.

_____ 4. He was also known as Hananiah.

_____ 5. He constructed an image of gold that was ninety feet high for the Babylonians to worship.

_____ 6. He was the best dream interpreter in Babylon.

_____ 7. He was also known as Mishael.

_____ 8. He survived an entire night in a den of hungry lions.

_____ 9. After being driven from Babylon, he became a wild creature, growing long hair and nails and eating grass like cattle.

_____ 10. He was also known as Azariah.

_____ 11. He was tossed into a blazing furnace for refusing to bow down to an idol.

_____ 12. He was killed after seeing mysterious fingers write a message on a wall during a banquet.

_____ 13. He issued a decree that all prayers should be offered to him.

_____ 14. He dreamed of four beasts.

_____ 15. He was the leader of Babylon when Judah was captured and the Israelites were taken into captivity.

DANIEL 2

Dream Reader

King Nebuchadnezzar has a puzzling dream and wants it interpreted. When his astrologers can't do it, the king orders that all of the wise men in Babylon—including Daniel and his friends—be executed. God reveals the dream and its interpretation to Daniel, who passes the information on to the king. The dream involves a giant statue made of various materials. Daniel explains that the dream represents the rise and fall of various earthly kingdoms and the ultimate triumph of God's kingdom. The king is so grateful for the dream interpretation that he promotes Daniel and his friends to high positions in his government.

Hand out copies of the reproducible sheet, "Math Confusion." Have kids form teams to work on the sheet. See how long it takes for kids to figure out that the problems are unsolvable because each one is missing a crucial piece of information. (For #1, you need to know how wide the pool is. For #2, you need to know how many guys are in the youth group. For #3, you need to know how many minutes it takes for Kent to read a chapter. For #4, you need to know the size of the fifth youth group.) Afterward, ask: **What would you do if your life depended on your ability to solve one of these problems?** Point out that Daniel faced a similar situation.

DATE I USED THIS SESSION _____ GROUP I USED IT WITH _____

NOTES FOR NEXT TIME _____

_____

_____

1. What's the weirdest dream you've ever had? More specifically, what's the weirdest dream you've ever had that you can share with this group?

2. Do you think all dreams have specific interpretations? In other words, do you think each of your dreams has a certain meaning? Explain.

3. Read Daniel 2:1-6. **Based on this passage, how would you describe King Nebuchadnezzar?** (He was troubled, disturbed by his dreams. He was a demanding employer, asking his wise men to do the impossible. He was impatient, demanding results right away. He was prone to poor judgment, using sorcerers and astrologers as advisers.)

4. **If you'd been one of the king's wise men, how do you think you would have felt about the king's challenge? Explain.** (The king's magicians, enchanters, sorcerers, and astrologers probably felt helpless, realizing that there was no way they could figure out what the king had dreamed.) **What does the wise men's response** (2:7-11) **tell you about them?** (They may have been con artists, offering the king phony advice and dream interpretations. When their skills were really tested, they admitted that what the king asked was impossible for them.)

5. **After asking the king for time to interpret the dream, what's the first thing that Daniel did** (2:17, 18)**?** (He consulted with his friends and asked them to pray.) **In what kinds of situations do you ask your friends for help? What kind of help might you ask for? Why?**

6. **What does Daniel's praise to God** (2:20-23) **tell us about God?** (God is involved in earthly events, setting up and deposing kings. All knowledge and wisdom come from God. He reveals hidden, secret things to His people.)

7. **Based on Daniel's attitude before the king in Daniel 2:24-30, if you had to sum up Daniel's character in one word, what would it be?** ("Humble" might be a good word. After all, Daniel is very careful to give God all of the glory for the interpretation of the dream. He also claims to be no wiser than any of the other wise men in the king's service.)

8. Read Daniel 2:31-35. **How would you interpret King Nebuchadnezzar's dream?** Encourage group members to be creative in their interpretations. Then compare their responses with the actual interpretation in Daniel 2:36-45.

9. How do you think the Jewish people in Daniel's time who heard about this dream and interpretation might have felt about it? (It may have been comforting to know that in spite of their exile, God was still in control and would still establish His kingdom forever, just as He had promised.)

10. Based on Nebuchadnezzar's comments in Daniel 2:47, how would you describe his view of and relationship with God? (He rightly recognizes God's power, but He doesn't acknowledge God as the one true God. He also doesn't place His trust in God and worship Him alone.)

Point out that Daniel describes the Lord as one who "reveals deep and hidden things" (2:22) and as the "God in heaven who reveals mysteries" (2:28). Hand out paper and pencils. Ask group members to write down one "deep and hidden thing" or one "mystery" that they would like God to reveal to them. If they can't think of one for themselves, ask them to write down one mystery that a non-Christian might like to have revealed. After a few minutes, collect the sheets and read the responses aloud. Encourage group members to comment on any of the mysteries that interest them. Close the session by explaining that though God may not reveal these mysteries immediately, we can rest assured that they will be answered some day. In the meantime, though, we can pray for a sense of peace about them.

MATH Confusion

After glancing at the problems on this sheet, you may be saying to yourself, "No way. I don't do math stuff outside of school." But we're asking you to make this one exception. Read the story problems below and come up with a solution for each one. The first team to correctly solve all four problems receives a **f a n t a b u l o u s** *prize.*

1. School's almost out, and Charles is ready to fill his family's swimming pool for the summer. The pool's actual depth is six feet, but Charles' dad likes to keep one foot of the pool unfilled. The length of the pool is 12 feet. So how many cubic feet of water will Charles need to fill the pool according to his dad's specifications? (Cubic measurement is found by taking length times width times height.)

2. Maria, one of six girls in her youth group, is bringing hot dogs for a cookout. She figures that after hiking and games, everyone will be hungry. She estimates that each girl will eat two hot dogs and that the guys will eat twice as many hot dogs as the girls do. Figuring in two hot dogs for the youth group leader, how many hot dogs should Maria bring?

3. Kent is a slow reader, but he wants to read through the entire Bible in one year. He knows that there are 913 chapters in the Old Testament and 260 in the New Testament. He would like to read something from the Bible every day. How many minutes should Kent read each day?

4. Melissa is in charge of renting buses for a retreat involving youth groups from five churches. Each bus holds 40 people. Melissa's youth group has two dozen members. Two of the other groups are twice as big as Melissa's; one is half that size. Figuring two adults for every dozen kids, how many buses does Melissa need?

DANIEL 3

Not Gonna Bow

King Nebuchadnezzar has an enormous image of gold constructed on the plain of Dura in Babylon. He assembles all of his government officials for the dedication of the image and commands that they bow down and worship the idol. Shadrach, Meshach, and Abednego—Daniel's friends from Israel—refuse to bow down. As a result, they are thrown into a fiery furnace. But much to the king's surprise, Shadrach, Meshach, and Abednego are not consumed by the fire. In fact, they emerge from the furnace completely unscathed. When the king sees this, he proclaims God's greatness.

(Needed: Building blocks, books)

Begin the session with a tower-building contest. Have kids form teams. Give each team a supply of building blocks. Explain that the teams will be competing to see which one can build the sturdiest tower. Give the teams a few minutes to work. When everyone is finished, "test" each tower by placing books on it one at a time. The tower that can withstand the most pressure—the one that supports the most books—is the winner. Afterward, use the idea of withstanding pressure to introduce the story of Shadrach, Meshach, and Abednego.

DATE I USED THIS SESSION _____ GROUP I USED IT WITH _____

NOTES FOR NEXT TIME _____

_____

_____

1. What's the most pressure you've ever faced in your life? What were the circumstances? How did you react? How did the situation turn out?

2. At the end of Daniel 2, King Nebuchadnezzar affirmed that God is the "God of gods and the Lord of kings" (2:47). But in Daniel 3, the king erects an idol for the Babylonians to worship (3:1-5). What's the deal? Why do you think the king forgot about God? (Perhaps Nebuchadnezzar's attitude was "What have you done for me lately?" Without seeing evidence of God's great power, he had a tendency to revert back to idol worship. Besides, nowhere in Daniel 2 does the king acknowledge the Lord as the *only* God.)

3. What do you think might cause a person like Nebuchadnezzar to set up a gold image and then command people to worship it under penalty of death?

4. Describe what you think Nebuchadnezzar's gold image looked like.

5. Do you think the king's officials really worshiped the image of gold or just pretended to (3:4-7)? Explain.

6. List some of the circumstances that might have made Shadrach, Meshach, and Abednego's decision (3:12) **difficult.** (There was a death sentence for anyone who refused to bow down to the image. There was "peer pressure" from all of the other officials who bowed down to the image. All three Israelites had bright futures in the king's government—futures that would most definitely be jeopardized by their decision.)

7. Why was King Nebuchadnezzar so angry with Shadrach, Meschach, and Abednego (3:13)? (By disobeying the king's command and refusing to worship his image, the three were not showing Nebuchadnezzar the respect he felt he deserved.)

8. Read Daniel 3:16-18. **Why would Shadrach, Meshach, and Abednego make such an extreme decision if they**

weren't even sure that God would protect them? (For all they knew, it may have been God's will for them to die as martyrs. But they knew that whatever God had in store for them was preferable to worshiping idols.)

9. **How do you think Shadrach, Meshach, and Abednego felt as they watched the furnace being heated seven times hotter than usual** (3:19)? **Explain.**

10. **Who was the fourth person in the fire** (3:25)? (It may have been an angel—or it may have been an appearance of the Lord Himself.)

11. **What do you think of Nebuchadnezzar's proclamation concerning God** (3:28, 29)? **Explain.** See Daniel 2:47. (Even though Nebuchadnezzar recognizes the superiority of Israel's God and threatens anyone who speaks against Him, the king never personally acknowledges God as Lord.)

Acknowledge that most people today aren't asked to bow down to golden images and don't face the prospect of being thrown into a fiery furnace. However, today's teenagers do face situations that may require them to take a public stand. Hand out copies of the reproducible sheet, "Take a Stand." Have kids form three teams. Assign one of the situations on the sheet to each team. Instruct each team to read its situation, suggest a possible course of action, and brainstorm a list of consequences—both good and bad—that might result from taking a stand. After a few minutes, have each team share its responses. Then discuss as a group whether the benefits of taking a public stand for God outweigh the possible negative consequences. As you wrap up the session, encourage group members to remember the story of the fiery furnace the next time they're faced with the prospect of taking a public stand for God.

TAKE A STAND

SITUATION 1

Your history teacher is talking about how cultures have changed over the years, moving away from "superstitious beliefs in otherworldly beings" and toward a rational, scientific understanding of the world. Although he keeps saying, "I don't mean to question any religious beliefs you may hold," it's obvious from the tone of his voice that that's exactly what he's trying to do. At the end of his lecture, he says to the class, "Now I'd like to hear *your* views on the subject." But everyone knows that if you try to disagree with him, he'll make you look like a fool. As a Christian, you disagree with the teacher's view. How should you respond?

SITUATION 2

For the first time ever, you're invited to eat lunch at the popular kids' table. You're a little nervous at first, but gradually you start to feel comfortable with this new group. You even manage to get off a pretty funny remark about the cafeteria food that sends the entire table into fits of laughter. Two of the people sitting across from you even smile and nod their heads approvingly to let you know that you've been accepted. You feel great. But then, about five minutes before the lunch period ends, one of the people at your table starts making fun of a couple guys sitting at another table. Pretty soon, another person at your table joins in—and then another. The comments keep getting worse and worse—making fun of the guys' clothes, questioning their sexuality, and so forth. As a Christian, you don't feel you should be a part of such conversations. What should you do?

SITUATION 3

You and your friends plan a week-long trip to the city during summer vacation. While in the city, you get tickets to attend the taping of a TV talk show. The topic of the show is abortion. Several pro-choice advocates on the panel state their positions clearly and persuasively. A few of the more radical advocates characterize pro-lifers as narrow-minded religious fanatics trying to restrict women's rights. One of the panelists even starts making fun of the Bible. The talk-show host opens the floor for audience response. As a Christian, you're offended by some of the remarks made by the panelists and by the stereotypical depictions of Christians. What should you do?

DANIEL 4

Neb's Nadir

After acknowledging God's greatness on two separate occasions in the past, King Nebuchadnezzar once again loses sight of God's power. Ignoring a warning he received in a dream, the king attempts to take credit for the greatness of Babylon. As a result, God forces him to live like a wild animal for a while. When the king finally comes to his senses and glorifies God, he is restored to the throne.

Begin the session with a game of volleyball. At some point during the game when one team is comfortably ahead of the other, give the losing team an opportunity to win the game. For instance, if Team A is ahead 11-3, announce just before Team B serves that the next point is worth 12 points. In other words, do whatever you can to insure that Team B wins the game. Afterward, see how the members of Team B respond to their victory. Ask: **Are you proud of your accomplishment? What do you think was the key moment in the game—the one that sealed your victory?** If the kids are honest, they'll admit that your altered scoring system won the game for them, and that they had little to do with the victory. Introduce your study of Daniel 4 by explaining that King Nebuchadnezzar refused to give credit where credit was due—and paid a severe penalty for it.

DATE I USED THIS SESSION _____ GROUP I USED IT WITH _____

NOTES FOR NEXT TIME _____

_____

_____

1. What accomplishment in your life are you most proud of? Why?

2. If someone asked you to talk about the amazing things that God has done for you (4:2), what would you say?

3. King Nebuchadnezzar has a dream (4:5). At least once before, Daniel was able to interpret a dream of the king when none of the other wise men in Babylon could (2:24-45). So why do you suppose the king first turns to his "magicians, enchanters, astrologers and diviners" (4:7) to interpret this dream? (Perhaps this indicates that the king wasn't completely convinced of the power of Daniel's God.)

4. Read the description of Nebuchadnezzar's dream in Daniel 4:10-17. Assuming that the tree represents King Nebuchadnezzar himself, how would you interpret the king's dream? Compare group members' responses with Daniel's interpretation in Daniel 4:19-27.

5. What does Daniel 4:18 tell you about King Nebuchadnezzar's spiritual condition? (He didn't acknowledge the Lord as the only God. He refers to Daniel's "gods.")

6. Why do you suppose Daniel was "perplexed" and "terrified" by the interpretation of the king's dream (4:19)? (Perhaps he was uncertain about how to break the bad news to Nebuchadnezzar.)

7. If you'd been King Nebuchadnezzar, how would you have responded to Daniel's interpretation of your dream (4:19-27)? Why?

8. Review some of the signs and wonders that Nebuchadnezzar had witnessed—specifically the interpretation of his first dream by Daniel and the salvation of Shadrach, Meshach, and Abednego in the fiery furnace. (See Daniel 2–3.) Why do you think Nebuchadnezzar seemed to forget about God's power again (4:29, 30)? What might cause people to forget about God's power today? Explain.

9. Read Daniel 4:31-33. If you were making a movie

about this incident in King Nebuchadnezzar's life, how would you make him look after the "transformation scene"?

10. What did Nebuchadnezzar have to do in order to be made "normal" again and restored to his throne (4:34-37)? (Praise God and acknowledge His power.)

11. Do you think King Nebuchadnezzar learned his lesson from this incident? Why or why not?

12. What can we learn about God from this passage? **Explain.** (God controls history and human affairs. He humbles the proud. If we repent, God is faithful to forgive our sins.)

(Needed: Prize)

Hand out copies of the reproducible sheet, "Accomplishments." Explain that the game is played like bingo—the first person to collect four initials in a row, whether vertical, horizontal, or diagonal, is the winner. Each group member may initial a sheet only once. Give kids a few minutes to collect initials. Afterward, award a prize to the winner. Then ask: **Do you think it's wrong to be proud of these accomplishments? Why or why not? How can we keep from getting into the kind of "pride trouble" that Nebuchadnezzar got in?** Emphasize the importance of acknowledging and thanking God for the primary role He plays in the things we accomplish. Close the session by giving kids an opportunity to acknowledge and thank God in prayer for what He's done for them.

ACCOMPLISHMENTS

The object of this game is to find people in your group who've accomplished the following things. When you find these people, have them initial the appropriate boxes. The first person to collect four initials in a row, whether vertical, horizontal, or diagonal, is the winner.

Played a leading role in a school play	Won a music competition	Been elected to class office	Had something published in a newspaper, yearbook, or magazine
Won a race	Received a citizenship or community service award	Earned an award at work, such as "Employee of the Month"	Made the starting lineup on a sports team
Earned a "perfect attendance" award	Made the school honor roll	Got an "A" on the last test he or she took	Had his or her picture in a newspaper
Won a trophy, medal, or ribbon	Had a drawing or piece of art displayed in public	Earned a badge in a club such as Boy Scouts, Girl Scouts, or Awana	Won a spelling bee

DANIEL 5

Babylonian Graffiti

King Belshazzar, a successor of Nebuchadnezzar, puts on a banquet for his nobles. The feast turns into a drunken orgy, during which the celebrants blaspheme God and praise idols. Suddenly, the fingers of a human hand appear and write a mysterious message on the palace wall. When no one can interpret the message, the king sends for Daniel. Daniel informs Belshazzar that, according to the message, the king's reign will be brought to an end and that Babylon will be given to the Medo-Persian Empire. That very night, Daniel's prediction comes true when Belshazzar is killed.

(Needed: Charade slips)

Prepare several slips of paper by writing on each slip an instruction that God might give—"Resist the devil," "Pray continually," "Read the Bible," "Love your enemies," etc. One at a time, have kids draw a slip of paper and act out the instruction. The catch is that the clue giver may use *only his or her arms and hands* to act out the instruction. When an instruction is guessed, the person who guessed it becomes the next clue giver. Continue until all of the slips have been used. Afterward, point out that in Daniel 5, God used an even more unconventional method of communication.

DATE I USED THIS SESSION _____ GROUP I USED IT WITH _____

NOTES FOR NEXT TIME _____

_____

_____

1. What's the most mysterious thing you've ever seen? How did it make you feel? Why?

2. What can we learn about King Belshazzar from the first four verses of Daniel 5? (He was a partier. He had no respect for the things of God. He worshiped idols.)

3. If you'd been a guest at Belshazzar's party, what would you have done when you saw the mystery hand appear (5:5)? Why?

4. Once again, we see that the king's enchanters, astrologers, and diviners were unable to interpret a message for the king (5:7, 8). See also Daniel 2:1-11; 4:4-7. **Why do you think the kings of Babylon consulted these guys?**

5. What was Daniel's reputation in Babylon (5:10-12)? (He was known as one "who has the spirit of the holy gods in him." He was "found to have insight and intelligence and wisdom like that of the gods." He also was known for his keen mind; his knowledge; his understanding; and his ability to interpret dreams, explain riddles, and solve difficult problems.)

6. How do you think Daniel would have responded if he'd heard the queen's description of him in Daniel 5:10-12? Why? (It's likely that Daniel would have given all of the glory to God for his abilities.)

7. Why do you think Daniel refused the king's gifts for interpreting the writing on the wall (5:17)? (Perhaps he didn't want to be obligated to anyone but the Lord.)

8. How would you compare King Belshazzar with his predecessor, King Nebuchadnezzar (5:18-23)? (Both kings were full of pride, but Nebuchadnezzar eventually learned humility [4:34-37].)

9. After Daniel interpreted the writing on the wall—which contained terrible news for King Belshazzar—the king rewards Daniel and promotes him in the kingdom. Doesn't that seem like an odd response? Why do you

think the king did that? (Perhaps he was simply fulfilling the promise he made in Daniel 5:7. Perhaps he was trying to appease the Lord by showing special favor to Daniel. Perhaps he didn't take Daniel's interpretation seriously, but was impressed with Daniel.)

10. **What does Daniel 5:30, 31 tell us about God?** (He keeps His Word. Sometimes His judgment is swifter than we imagine. He punishes the wicked. He is powerful enough to control the affairs of nations.)

(Needed: Chalkboard and chalk or newsprint and marker)

Hand out copies of the reproducible sheet, "The Message." Give group members a few minutes to complete the sheet. When everyone is finished, ask volunteers to write the messages they came up with on the board. Then have them explain the messages and predict how the people at the party might respond. As you wrap up the session, ask group members to identify at least one area in their life in which they aren't honoring God. Then give them a few minutes to consider some ways they might begin to honor God in that area. Encourage kids to address such situations now, before God sends a more *serious* message to them.

THE MESSAGE

Some of the kids at your school have what they call a **"Weekly Blow Out."** Every Friday night, they gather at a secret location to "party their brains out." Only a few select people know the location of the party, and they're sworn to secrecy. You've never been invited because you're a Christian. But from what you've heard, the "Weekly Blow Out" can get pretty wild. According to the rumors, all kinds of weird things go on at these parties—not just drinking, drugs, and sex, but also things like séances and "Ouija" board games.

One Friday night around 11:30, you get a call from a non-Christian friend at the "Weekly Blow Out." He sounds a little drunk and very upset. "You've gotta get over here right away," he yells into the phone. **"You're the only one who can help us.** We don't know what to do!" But rather than telling you what's going on, he gives you directions to the party and hangs up.

At first, you consider just ignoring the call. But your friend was pretty upset. So after explaining the situation to your parents, you take off. When you get to the house where the party is being held, you find that everyone is anxiously waiting for you. Most of the people look stoned or drunk—and very scared.

Your friend grabs you by the arm and drags you into the living room. "We were just partying and having a good time," he explains, "when this giant hand appeared out of nowhere and wrote something on the wall. Don't laugh—but I think it was God's hand." Other people nod their heads vigorously in agreement.

On the opposite side of the living room, written in letters at least seven feet high that look like they were burned into the wall, is a message from God.

What does the message say? (Is it a Bible reference? A mysterious warning from God? The name of a Bible character who was punished by God for wickedness?) How would you explain the message to the people at the party? How do you think they would respond?

DANIEL 6

The Prayer Dare

OVERVIEW

The Babylonian Empire has been defeated by the Medes and the Persians. Darius is now the ruler over Babylon. But Daniel still holds a high government position. Daniel's appointment causes jealousy among some of the other officials, and they set a trap for him. By appealing to King Darius's pride, they convince him to forbid the worship of anyone but himself, with violators sentenced to be thrown into the lions' den. Undaunted, Daniel maintains his habit of daily prayers to God. He's discovered by the officials, who demand that he be punished. Daniel is thrown into the lions' den, but is protected by God and released unharmed the next morning.

OPENING ACT

One at a time, have kids come to the front of the room and imitate a distinctive habit of someone else in the group. It may be a physical habit (for example, drumming on a desk top) or a verbal habit (for example, using a favorite expression). See how long it takes for the rest of the group to figure out who's being imitated. Emphasize that the imitations should be harmless and good-natured—they *must not* be embarrassing for the person being imitated. If your kids don't know each other well, encourage them to do imitations of you or of celebrities. Afterward, explain that Daniel was known for a certain habit—one that almost got him killed.

DATE I USED THIS SESSION _____ GROUP I USED IT WITH _____

NOTES FOR NEXT TIME _____

_____

_____

1. **What things would you be willing to die for? Why?** Many kids may say they'd be willing to die for their family or their country or to save the life of another person. But how many of them would be willing to die for Christian principles?

2. **How do you think Daniel "distinguished himself" among the administrators and satraps of Babylon** (6:3)? (Daniel may have been well known for his wisdom, godliness, and dream interpretations when he served in the courts of Nebuchadnezzar and Belshazzar.) **How do you distinguish yourself from other people at your school? Explain.**

3. Read Daniel 6:4, 5. **Why do you think the administrators and satraps tried to find charges to bring against Daniel?** (It's likely that they were jealous of his position in the government.) **How do you think they felt when they couldn't find anything to charge Daniel with?**

4. **Have you ever felt like people were trying to find things wrong with you? If so—without naming names— what were the circumstances? What happened? How did you feel?**

5. **Why do you think King Darius fell for the scheme of the administrators and satraps** (6:6-9)? (They appealed to the king's pride and showered him with flattery.)

6. **If someone wanted to manipulate you into doing something you didn't really want to do, what would be the best approach? Why?**

7. **What does Daniel 6:10 tell us about the character of Daniel?** (He was courageous—after all, he knew that the decree had been issued when he went to his room to pray. He was honest and upright—he did not try to hide what he was doing. He had his priorities in order—his responsibilities to God took precedence over his responsibilities to the king. He was willing to die for his faith.)

8. Read Daniel 6:11-16. **What does this passage tell us about King Darius?** (He was bright enough to realize that he'd been tricked by the administrators and satraps. He seems to have genuinely cared about Daniel. He seems to have had at least some hope that God would be able to save Daniel.)

9. How do you think Daniel felt when he was thrown into the lions' den? Explain.

10. What if God had *not* saved Daniel from the lions, but instead allowed him to be killed? How might your attitude toward this story be different? Explain.

11. What is the moral of the story in Daniel 6?

12. Based on Daniel 6, would you say that there are some laws that Christians aren't required to obey? If so, which ones? If not, why not? How should a Christian respond to a law that he or she believes violates God's law?

Hand out copies of the reproducible sheet, "Dear Daniel." Let kids work in pairs or small groups to complete the sheet. If possible, make sure that each letter on the sheet is addressed by at least one group. Encourage kids to be specific in their advice and to use examples from Daniel's life as illustrations. After a few minutes, have each group read its letter and its response. Allow time for other group members to offer their comments and suggestions. Close the session in prayer, thanking God that He protects and takes care of us in the tough situations we face.

Dear Daniel

Read the letters below and choose one to answer. In answering it, imagine that you are Daniel. Give the advice you think he would give, making it as specific to the situation as possible. When possible, illustrate your advice with examples from Daniel's own life.

Dear Daniel,
The other day in the lunchroom, I started to bow my head to pray. One of the guys across the table saw me and started making fun of me. "You're not praying, are you?" he asked. Everyone at the table turned to look at me, and I got nervous. "No, I wasn't praying," I said as convincingly as possible. "I dropped one of my contacts." (To make matters worse, I don't even wear contacts!) I think everyone believed me, but now I feel terrible about it. What should I do?
                                                Timid in Topeka

Dear Daniel,
In health class yesterday, we had a guest speaker from a local medical clinic. She spoke about sexual responsibility and why abortion should not be ruled out as an option for pregnant women. She was a convincing speaker, and by the time she was finished, she had most of the class agreeing with her position. When she asked if we had any questions or comments, one of the girls in the class pointed at me and said, "She believes abortion is murder. She thinks it should be illegal." The speaker asked me to stand and explain my position. I got scared and said, "I don't really know what I believe. I haven't made up my mind yet." Since then, some non-Christian girls I hang around with have been saying that I'm becoming "one of them." I don't want to be thought of that way. What should I do?
                                                Big-Time Choke

Dear Daniel,
My grandparents are missionaries in Central Africa. About a month ago, two tribes in that area declared war on each other. The casualties from the war have been tremendous. My grandparents called last week to let us know that they're OK, even though they've had some close calls. We tried to urge them to come back to the states for a few months until the tensions ease, but they refused. Just last night, we heard that several missionaries have been targeted for attack. I'm worried that I'll never see my grandparents again. What should I do?

                                                Worried in Washington

DANIEL 7–12

Dreams and Visions

OVERVIEW

In Daniel 7–12, Daniel records his prophetic dreams and visions, which emphasize God's hand in history. These dreams and visions involve such images as four beasts, a ram and a goat, and a man with a face like lightning. Their interpretations deal with such issues as the rise and fall of future world empires, the coming Messiah, and the end times.

OPENING ACT

(Needed: Prizes)

Have kids form pairs. Send one person from each pair out of the room. Ask the remaining person in each pair to predict something about his or her partner. For instance, you might say: **Predict how many jumping jacks your partner can do in thirty seconds.** Write down each person's prediction. Then bring in the partners and give them thirty seconds to do as many jumping jacks as possible. Compare the number of jumping jacks done by each person with the number predicted by his or her partner. Award a point to the pair whose numbers are closest. Then send the other person from each pair out of the room and have his or her partner make a prediction about him or her. Play several rounds. Award prizes to the pair with the most points at the end of the game. Use this activity to introduce Daniel's predictions in Daniel 7–12.

DATE I USED THIS SESSION _____ GROUP I USED IT WITH _____

NOTES FOR NEXT TIME _____

_____

_____

1. If you knew what was going to happen in the future, how would you use that knowledge? Why?

2. Why do you think God used dreams and visions to communicate with Daniel? Why didn't He just *tell* Daniel what was going to happen in the future?

3. What do the four beasts represent in Daniel 7:3-8? (Most likely, they represent four empires or nations. The lion with eagle's wings probably represents the Babylonian Empire. The bear probably represents the Medo-Persian Empire. The winged leopard probably represents the Greek Empire of Alexander the Great. The beast with iron teeth probably represents the Roman Empire.)

4. Who is the "Ancient of Days" (7:9, 13, 22)? What does that name symbolize? (God is the Ancient of Days. The name refers to His eternal nature.)

5. When you hear God described as the Ancient of Days, what kind of mental picture do you get of Him? Why? Compare group members' responses with the description of God in Daniel 7:9, 10.

6. Who is the "son of man" (7:13)? What does the name symbolize? (Jesus is the Son of Man. In the Old Testament, "son of man" is just another term for humans [Psalm 8:4]. In the New Testament, "Son of Man" was Jesus' favorite title for Himself.)

7. How would you explain Daniel 7:14 to a non-Christian? Do you think this verse might cause a non-Christian to investigate Christianity a little more closely? Why or why not?

8. Daniel mentions being "appalled" by his vision of the ram and goat, and describes the vision itself as being "beyond understanding" (8:27). Why do you think Daniel had such a reaction to it? (Part of the vision involved things that would occur in the distant future [8:26]—perhaps things that were beyond Daniel's comprehension.)

9. According to Daniel 10:12, why was Daniel favored with such direct contact with God? (He set his mind to gain understanding and he humbled himself before God.) **Do you think these things might affect a person's relationship with God today? Explain.**

10. Hand out copies of the reproducible sheet, "Do-It-Yourself Prophecy." Let kids work in pairs or small groups to complete the sheet. After a few minutes, have each pair or small group share what it came up with. **What difference do Daniel's prophecies make in our lives today? Are there any principles we can learn from them? Explain.** (God is in control of history and knows exactly what will happen in the future. We can trust Him to protect and provide for us.)

Read Romans 8:38, 39 and Matthew 6:34. Discuss as a group what should be our attitude toward the future. The prophecies of Daniel make the future seem mysterious and threatening. Yet the Lord tells us not to worry about the future, that the future cannot affect our relationship with Him. Have kids form small groups. Instruct each group to come up with a rap, chant, slogan, song, or poem that communicates what the future means for Christians. After a few minutes, have each group share and explain its creation.

Do-It-Yourself Prophecy

You've read about some of Daniel's dreams and visions, so you know what's included in a good prophecy. It involves things like beasts that look like an animal cross-breeding experiment gone crazy, goats attacking rams, angels, men with faces like lightning and eyes like flaming torches, and so forth. With these images in mind, come up with a prophecy of your own, describing (in "prophetic" style) what you think the end times will be like. How will our age end? What will Jesus' return be like? You tell us.

HOSEA

For Better and for Worse

Hosea is told by God to take an adulterous wife, Gomer. After she is driven out because of her adultery, God tells Hosea to take her back again. God uses this relationship to illustrate His relationship with Israel, who is "disloyal" to Him time and time again, yet is taken back by Him time and time again.

(Needed: Tape)

Have kids form teams. Cut apart one copy of the reproducible sheet, "A Match Made in Heaven," for each team. Have the teams line up. On the opposite wall, tape one set of cards for each team. The first person in each line will run to his or her team's set of cards, choose a "matching pair," run back, and tape the cards to the wall next to the team. The first team to match all ten pairs is the winner. (The answers are as follows: Mr. Brady—Carol; Mr. Simpson—Marge; Mrs. Conner—Dan; Mrs. Petrie—Rob; Mrs. Bumstead—Dagwood; Mr. Howell—Lovey; Mr. Ricardo—Lucy; Mr. Washington—Martha; Abraham—Sarah; Hosea—Gomer.) Use this activity to introduce the relationship between Hosea and Gomer.

DATE I USED THIS SESSION _____ GROUP I USED IT WITH _____

NOTES FOR NEXT TIME _____

_____

_____

1. What are the four most important qualities you'll look for in a spouse? Why are those things important to you? Where does loyalty rank on your list? Why?

2. How would you react if you found out that your spouse—or even your boyfriend or girlfriend—was having a sexual relationship with someone else? Why? (The reaction of many people probably would be to end the relationship.)

3. Why do you think the Lord instructed Hosea, one of His own prophets, to marry Gomer, an adulterous woman (1:2)? (The Lord wanted this relationship to serve as an example of the "marriage" covenant between Himself and His bride, Israel, who was defiled.)

4. Hosea's marriage to Gomer probably caused Hosea a lot of heartache, grief, and embarrassment. Why do you think God chose such a method to communicate His message? (One of the best answers can be found in Ecclesiastes 11:5—"You cannot understand the work of God." In His infinite wisdom, God knew that the best way to communicate His truth to the Israelites was through a marital "object lesson.")

5. Hosea and Gomer had three kids. God instructed Hosea to give his kids some rather unusual names to reflect the status of Israel in the Lord's eyes (1:3-9). If God named kids today based on how He feels about our society's moral behavior, what might a school roll call sound like? Explain.

6. In Hosea 3:1, the Lord tells Hosea to take Gomer back, despite her adulterous ways. How does this represent the "marriage" of God and Israel? (While the people of Israel constantly "cheated" on God, looking for satisfaction from other gods, God took the Israelites back time and time again, forgiving their sins.)

7. If God is prepared to condemn and judge people for "stumbling" in sin (4:5; 5:5), what hope do we have? Romans 3:23 says, "For all have sinned, and fall short of

the glory of God." Are we in a no-win situation? Explain.
(The people of Israel were going to be judged not because of their sin, but because of their *unrepentant attitude* toward their sin [5:15; 7:14]. Those who repent of their sin and ask God for forgiveness will be forgiven.)

8. **God says in Hosea 6:6 that He desires "mercy, not sacrifice, and acknowledgment of God rather than burnt offerings." What do you think He's referring to?** (Instead of repenting and acknowledging the greatness of God by asking for forgiveness, the Israelites were simply going through the motions by offering sacrifices.)

9. **What are some "spiritual routines" that people today go through instead of sincerely repenting and asking for forgiveness? Explain.**

10. **Hosea 14:2 offers a seemingly simple solution to Israel's problem. Why do you think so many people have a hard time following these instructions?** (Some people may not feel sorry about what they've done and may not recognize the need for repentance. Others may think they've sinned so badly that they can't be forgiven.)

11. **Hosea speaks of God's punishment for Israel in chapters 9, 10, 12, and 13 before discussing in chapter 14 the blessings that will come after repentance. What does this say about the "sin-repentance-forgiveness" process?** (Even when we confess our sins before God and receive forgiveness from Him, there may still be consequences to be paid. God is just as well as loving. Such consequences serve as reminders of the painful effects of sin in our lives.)

As a group, briefly discuss how God must feel when we are "unfaithful" to Him. Then give kids an opportunity to silently consider some areas in which they've been unfaithful lately. Read I John 1:9. Emphasize God's willingness to forgive us—no matter what we've done. Close the session with a time of silent prayer, giving kids an opportunity to confess their unfaithfulness to God and receive His forgiveness.

A Match Made in Heaven

	Mr. Brady	Carol
	Mr. Simpson	Marge
	Mrs. Conner	Dan
	Mrs. Petrie	Rob
	Mrs. Bumstead	Dagwood
	Mr. Howell	Lovey
	Mr. Ricardo	Lucy
	Mr. Washington	Martha
	Abraham	Sarah
	Hosea	Gomer

JOEL

The Locust Invasion

An invasion of locusts and a severe drought have wreaked havoc on Judah. God tells His prophet Joel that these conditions mean more than just a bad harvest year; they are signs of the nearing day of the Lord, when God will judge all nations for their wickedness. Joel warns that the Israelites must repent before they can receive any of God's blessings.

(Needed: Four buckets, water, paper cups)

Have kids form two teams. Say: **You're Israelites during the time of Joel, and you're facing a severe drought. A couple of wells have been located, but they're drying up quickly.** Have the teams line up. On the opposite side of the room, place two buckets filled with water. Place an empty bucket next to each team. Then hand out paper cups. Have the teams compete to see which one can transfer—using the paper cups—the most water from its full bucket to its empty one in five minutes. Just before the game starts, however, announce that the land is being invaded by locusts. And since kids will need their hands to fight off the insects, they must carry their cups in their mouths. No one may use his or her hands at all during the contest. Afterward, measure each team's water level and declare a winner. Then discuss the Book of Joel.

DATE I USED THIS SESSION _____ GROUP I USED IT WITH _____

NOTES FOR NEXT TIME _____

_____

_____

1. What is your least favorite insect? Why? Have you ever had any bad experiences with insects? Explain.

2. What does a locust look like? What kinds of problems might a locust invasion cause? (A locust is a short-horned grasshopper. Locust swarms are very dangerous to agriculture because they can strip an area of all of its vegetation.)

3. Many passages in the Bible—like Daniel's vision of the ram and goat in Daniel 8—are symbolic. The characters and incidents represent other things and are not meant to be taken literally. Do you think the locusts described in Joel 1 are symbolic, or was Israel really in the middle of a bugfest? Explain.

4. The Israelites are called to mourn because of the drought and locust plague. This mourning involved things like putting on sackcloth, wailing, fasting, and crying out to God (1:13, 14). **Do you think we should approach God in a similar manner today when we come to Him in repentance? Why or why not?**

5. The drought and the invasion of the locusts were part of God's judgment on the people of Judah for their wickedness. Why do you think the people of Judah needed such extreme reminders of their sinfulness before they were willing to repent?

6. "The day of the Lord" is mentioned several times in the Book of Joel (1:15; 2:1, 11, 31; 3:14). **What do you think this phrase is referring to?** If no one mentions it, explain that the phrase appears several times in the prophetic books of the Bible. It's usually used to describe one of two things: God's direct intervention in history (such as the locust invasion in Joel) or Christ's return (at which time God's enemies will be punished and God's people will be rewarded).

7. Read Joel 2:28-32. **Describe what you think the day of the Lord will be like.**

8. In Joel 2:12-14, God offers the Israelites a ray of hope in the midst of this "calamity." What is it? (If the Israelites will return to the Lord and His ways, He may show pity on the people and relieve their suffering.)

9. What do you think the statement "Rend your heart and not your garments" means (2:13)? (God wanted the people's *sincere* repentance, not just a religious "show" of tearing their clothes in grief.)

10. What clues can we get from the Book of Joel as to what God is like? (He is just, requiring that sinfulness be punished. He loves His people, and will stop at nothing to get them to turn back to Him. He is merciful, willing to forgive even the worst of sins if only people will repent.)

Hand out copies of the reproducible sheet, "My Prayer." Give group members a few minutes to complete the sheet. Emphasize that no one else will see what group members write, so they should be honest in their responses. After a few minutes, read Joel 2:12, 13 as a reminder of the Lord's mercy and faithfulness. If there are non-Christians in your group, you might also want to read Joel 2:32; then encourage kids who want to know more about beginning a personal relationship with the Lord to talk with you after the session.

My Prayer

Lord,

Even though I may not be facing a locust swarm like the people of Judah were, I am facing some difficult situations that seem almost as devastating to me. Among the most difficult situations I'm facing right now are

_____

_____

_____ .

These situations are affecting me in the following ways: _____

_____

_____ .

I'm asking You to _____

_____

_____ .

My relationship with You right now is _____

because _____ .

In Joel 2:12, You say, "Return to me with all your heart." In order for me to return to You with all of my heart, I will need to _____

_____

_____ .

As I attempt to return to You with all of my heart, please help me to

_____

_____ .

AMOS

The Trial

While enjoying a time of prosperity and peace, the Israelites forget about their covenant with God. Their commitment to God involves nothing more than simply performing rituals, which they believe frees them to live however they choose. The Israelites are convinced that God will judge all other nations, but will bless them. God, through His prophet Amos, warns of impending destruction. He also makes it clear that He is Lord of all nations—and that He will *judge* all nations.

(Needed: List of stunts, play money)

Create a list of various stunts that kids can perform to "earn" play money. Assign different monetary values to the stunts, depending on the difficulty of each one. For instance, whistling a TV show theme might be worth $1; crawling around the room three times might be worth $5; memorizing the middle names of everyone in the group might be worth $10; etc. You'll need several different stunts for kids to choose from for each dollar amount. If a player completes a stunt, he or she receives the appropriate amount of money. The person with the most money at the end of the game is the winner. To introduce the Book of Amos, point out that the Israelites' pursuit of prosperity caused some serious problems.

DATE I USED THIS SESSION _____ GROUP I USED IT WITH _____

NOTES FOR NEXT TIME _____

_____

_____

1. Think of a famous trial that's going on right now. Do you think the defendant is guilty or not guilty? Why? If you think the defendant is guilty, what kind of punishment do you think he or she should receive? Why?

2. Amos 1–2 seems to be describing a courtroom trial, with God as the judge. Who's on trial? What are the charges? What kinds of sentences does God hand down? (The enemies of Israel—Aram, Philistia, Phoenicia, Edom, Ammon, and Moab—are on trial. They are charged with offenses such as mistreating captives, idolatry, and burning the bones of a conquered king. God's sentences involve fire consuming the nations' fortresses and military defeat.)

3. Punishment isn't limited to the enemy nations of Israel, however. Both Judah and Israel are charged by God during "the trial." What are some things they're being tried for (2:4-16)? (Rejecting the law of the Lord, being led astray by false gods, selling the righteous for silver, sexual immorality.)

4. If the Israelites were God's chosen people, why would He pour out His wrath on them (2:4, 6)? (God's holiness demands that sin be punished. Besides, the Lord disciplines those He loves [Proverbs 3:12].)

5. In Amos 4:6-11, God offers several examples of things He allowed the Israelites to face so they would return to Him for strength. What are some of the things He mentions? (Hunger, drought, locusts, plagues, etc.) Why do you think the Israelites still refused to turn to God?

6. Which of the things mentioned by God would be most effective in causing you to turn back to Him? Explain.

7. Do you think God still allows bad things to happen to people today to turn their attention back to Him? Why or why not?

8. God's instruction in Amos 5:14 seems pretty simple. So why is it so hard to "seek good, not evil"?

9. In Amos 5:21-23, God proclaims His hatred for the Israelites' religious feasts, worship assemblies, offerings, and songs to Him. Why do you think God feels this way? (The Israelites were simply going through the motions, performing the rituals out of habit. In other words, their hearts weren't in it.) **How do you think God feels today when people treat going to church, singing hymns, giving offerings, and praying as rituals done out of habit? Explain.**

10. Amos 6:1–9:10 speaks of the impending destruction of Israel. But then the grim Book of Amos closes with God's speaking of the restoration of Israel. What's with God's change of heart? (God's heart is unchanging—He is always loving and merciful; but He is also a just and righteous God who will allow no blessings until we've repented and asked forgiveness for our wickedness.)

(Needed: Newspapers or newsmagazines, chalkboard and chalk or newsprint and marker)

Hand out copies of the reproducible sheet, "Same As It Ever Was." Let kids work in pairs or small groups to complete the sheet. Make available some newspapers or newsmagazines for kids to refer to as they work. After a few minutes, have each pair or group share its responses. Afterward, focus your attention on some of the social injustices listed by group members. Read Amos 5:11-13. Then discuss as a group ways that Christians can call attention to and attempt to rectify social injustices in our society. Create a list on the board of group members' suggestions. Then have each person choose one idea from the list that he or she will attempt within the next two weeks. Plan a time at a future meeting for kids to share their results.

SAME AS IT EVER WAS

During Amos' ministry, both Israel (the northern kingdom) and Judah (the southern kingdom) enjoyed great prosperity. Some had prophesied that Israel would become powerful again, so the people of Israel were convinced that they were in God's good graces. But as Israel became more prosperous, it also became more corrupt—both religiously and morally.

Unfortunately, the more things change, the more they stay the same. Many people today believe that our society is becoming more and more corrupt. In fact, our society has quite a bit in common with ancient Israel.

Below are four categories of corruption found in ancient Israel. For each category, see if you can come up with some specific modern-day examples of corruption in our society.

Government Corruption

Oppression of the Poor

Immorality

Idolatry (Misplaced Priorities)

OBADIAH

What Comes Around Goes Around

The Edomites, descendants of Esau, are longtime enemies of the Israelites, descendants of Jacob. After Israel is conquered by foreign nations, the Edomites gloat in their own security and in Israel's destruction. God is displeased that the Edomites, who are relatives of the Israelites, didn't come to the aid of the Israelites. Instead, the Edomites fought *against* the Israelites. Through His prophet Obadiah, God warns the Edomites of impending destruction for their actions.

(Needed: Tennis ball, radio or tape player)

Have kids form a circle. Ask one person to sit away from the circle, starting and stopping music. Hand a tennis ball to one of the kids in the circle. Explain that when the music starts, he or she must pass the ball to the person on his or her right. That person will then pass the ball to the next person, and so on. When the music stops, the person holding the ball is out. Continue until only one person remains. Use this activity to introduce the idea that "what comes around goes around"—a point that God makes very clear in the Book of Obadiah.

DATE I USED THIS SESSION _____ GROUP I USED IT WITH _____

NOTES FOR NEXT TIME _____

_____

_____

1. When you hear that someone is having a difficult time in his or her life, are you more likely to (a) offer to help that person or (b) secretly rejoice that it's him or her having the problem, and not you? Why? What if the person having the problem was your worst enemy? How would you react?

2. The Edomites were descendants of Esau; the Israelites were descendants of Jacob. Why do you think these two groups of people, who were related to each other, had such a history of hostility toward each other? See Genesis 25:19-34; 27:1-46. (Esau sold his birthright to Jacob for some food. Later, Jacob tricked Esau out of their father's blessing. This legacy of deception and mistrust was passed on from generation to generation.)

3. During the time of Obadiah's writing, Israel had been conquered by a foreign nation. So why is God angry at the Edomites (Obadiah 1-4)? (They gloated over Israel's destruction. They prided themselves in the fact that they were "invincible" in their mountain stronghold.)

4. What kinds of things might cause people today to feel invincible? Explain.

5. Obadiah 10, 11 gives a more complete picture of the Edomites' offense against Israel. In addition to gloating over Israel's destruction, what else were the Edomites guilty of? (Actually helping the invaders attack and conquer Israel.)

6. Why were the actions of the Edomites especially revolting to God (10-14)? (In essence, the Edomites were fighting against their own blood relatives—blood relatives who happened to be God's chosen people.)

7. Do you think God's words in Obadiah 10-14 apply to family situations today? If so, how? If not, why not?

8. How would you explain the principle of Obadiah 15 to a five year old? What kind of illustrations might you use?

9. What are some specific areas of a teenager's life that might be affected by the principle of Obadiah 15? (His or her attitude toward friends, "outsiders" or unpopular people, and members of the opposite sex.)

10. "Poetic justice" is an outcome in which a person receives what he or she deserves in a manner that is especially ironic or appropriate. For instance, poetic justice for a man who taunts disabled people might involve his being disabled in an accident. What would be poetic justice for the Edomites? Explain. Compare group members' responses with God's pronouncement of judgment in Obadiah 15-21.

Hand out copies of the reproducible sheet, "Paybacks." Let group members work in pairs to complete the sheet. After a few minutes, have group members share their responses. Then discuss as a group whether any of the immediate positive results of the actions listed on the sheet are worth the eventual negative consequences. Emphasize that even though it sometimes seems like wicked people get away with their sins, the Edomites serve as a reminder that God will eventually punish such people or allow them to suffer the consequences of their sins.

There's nothing better than a good "payback," is there? Words can't describe the satisfaction of watching the kids who just cut in line in front of you at the roller coaster being "escorted" out of the park. But what about the times when those people cutting in line in front of you get away with it? That's when life just doesn't seem fair. The Edomites probably felt like successful line cutters—invincible, believing that nothing could happen to them. But their actions eventually caught up with them. Sometimes it may seem that God allows people to get away with sinful actions, but we can rest assured that they will eventually face the consequences for what they do.

For each action listed below, list some possible positive results (for the person responsible for the action) and some possible negative consequences.

	Positive Results	Negative Consequences
Cheating on a test		
Spreading a rumor about someone at school		
Having a beer or two like everyone else at Friday night's party		
Going too far sexually		
Telling a racist joke		
Making fun of a new kid at school for the way he or she dresses		
Lying to an employer about being sick in order to go to a concert with friends		
Using a few swear words while goofing around with friends		
Sneaking out after curfew to see a midnight movie with friends		

JONAH 1–2

A Fishy Story

OVERVIEW

God tells Jonah to go to Nineveh to preach. Instead, Jonah boards a ship bound for Tarshish. God sends a violent storm that threatens to destroy the ship. To appease God, the sailors throw Jonah into the sea, where he is swallowed by a great fish. Inside the fish, Jonah prays to God. After three days and nights, the fish vomits Jonah onto dry land.

OPENING ACT

Begin the session with a game of "Reverse Simon Says." Lead the group in a traditional game of "Simon Says"—with one twist: Each time you give a command that's preceded by "Simon says," group members must do the *opposite* of what you say. For instance, if you say, **Simon says close your right eye,** players must close their left eye. If you say, **Simon says sit on a chair,** group members must stand on a chair. If a group member messes up, he or she is out. Play a couple of rounds, as time allows. Afterward, point out that the prophet Jonah probably would have been good at this game—after all, he practiced doing the opposite of what God told him to do.

DATE I USED THIS SESSION _____ GROUP I USED IT WITH _____

NOTES FOR NEXT TIME _____

_____

_____

1. What's the worst trouble you've ever gotten into as a result of disobeying a parent or some other authority figure?

2. Let's say that while you're lying in your bed tonight, God tells you to go into the heart of New York City to start preaching against it. What would you do? Why?

3. What kind of "wickedness" (1:2) do you think was going on in Nineveh to make the Lord single out that city for judgment?

4. Why do you think Jonah "ran away from the Lord" (1:3)? Do you suppose he really thought he could get away from God? Explain. (Perhaps he was just trying to postpone his responsibilities, hoping that God would change His mind.)

5. Why didn't Jonah want to go to Nineveh to preach? See Jonah 4:2. (The Ninevites were bitter enemies of the Israelites. Jonah was afraid that if he preached to the Ninevites, they might repent and be spared by God. [As it turns out, that's exactly what happened.] Jonah wanted the Ninevites to be destroyed by God.)

6. Are there any commands in God's Word that you would rather not obey if you were given a choice? If so, which ones? Explain. ("Love your enemies" [Matthew 5:44] can be a pretty distasteful command to some people.)

7. Read Jonah 1:4-12. **Imagine that you're one of the sailors on Jonah's ship. You're in the midst of a violent storm. Your ship is coming apart. You find out that all of this is happening because one of the passengers on the ship is running away from God. This passenger tells you that the only way to escape the storm is to throw him overboard—but that would be murder. What would you do? Why?** Compare group members' responses with the sailors' actions in Jonah 1:13-16.

8. Do you think Jonah believed the Lord would save him when he told the sailors to throw him into the sea? Why or why not? (It's likely that Jonah believed he was going to die because of his disobedience. Perhaps he even preferred death to the alternative of preaching to the Ninevites.)

9. **Imagine that you're Jonah. You've been caught trying to run away from God, thrown into a raging sea, and swallowed by a fish (1:17). Now you've got a few days inside the fish to do some soul-searching. What kinds of things might you be thinking about at this point? Why?**

10. Read Jonah 2:1-9. **What does Jonah's prayer tell us about how Jonah was feeling inside the fish?** (More than anything else, Jonah was grateful to be alive—especially after he disobeyed God.)

11. **Describe what you think Jonah looked like after being vomited by the fish (2:10).**

Hand out copies of the reproducible sheet, "What's It Going to Take?" Give group members a few minutes to complete the sheet. When everyone is finished, ask volunteers to share their ideas. Discuss as a group why some people refuse to obey or even listen to God until they experience dire circumstances (like being trapped in the belly of a fish). Ask: **Can you think of some areas in your life in which you've been—or are being—disobedient to God? How might God be trying to get your attention concerning those areas? What will He have to do before you take care of the situation?** Ask group members to pray about the areas of their lives in which they've been or are being disobedient. Encourage kids to ask God for His help in becoming obedient to Him.

What's It Going TO TAKE?

God used a great fish to focus Jonah's attention on his disobedience. But sometimes God uses less . . . dramatic methods to get people's attention. What methods might God use to get the attention of the following people?

A young person who sometimes goes on vandalism sprees "just for the fun of it"

A young person who makes a habit of saying crude and offensive things

A young person who refuses to obey his or her parents, flaunting his or her independence at every opportunity

A young person who starts drinking alcohol in order to fit in with a certain group at school

A Christian young person who secretly collects pornographic magazines and videos

A Christian young person who is dating someone that he or she knows is "bad news"

JONAH 3–4

A Reluctant Prophet

After getting Jonah's attention with the fish incident, God again commands Jonah to go to Nineveh. This time, Jonah obeys. He warns the Ninevites that their city will be destroyed in forty days. The Ninevites take Jonah's words to heart and repent of their wickedness. As a result, God refrains from destroying Nineveh. This angers Jonah, who is upset at God's compassion for Israel's enemies. He sulks outside the city, waiting for it to be destroyed. The Book of Jonah concludes with an affirmation of God's concern for all people.

(Needed: Slips of paper, container)

Write on separate slips of paper things that kids might gripe about—curfew, gym class, liver and onions, family vacations, etc. One at a time, have volunteers draw a slip and complain about the topic. However, the person may not say any of the words that appear on the slip. For example, a person complaining about liver and onions might say, "Mom, I hate that slimy kind of meat—especially when you serve it with that vegetable that makes people cry." The object is to get the rest of the group to guess what you're complaining about without using the words on the slip. Afterward, explain that you're going to look at a prophet who was a champion complainer.

DATE I USED THIS SESSION _____ GROUP I USED IT WITH _____

NOTES FOR NEXT TIME _____

_____

_____

1. What kinds of things do you complain about most? Why?

2. Imagine that you're Jonah. You've just been vomited onto shore after spending three days in the belly of a fish for refusing to go to Nineveh as God commanded you to do. Now God commands you once again to go to Nineveh (3:1, 2). What do you do? Why?

3. Imagine that you're a citizen of Nineveh. A strange, bleached-looking man with a rather pungent fishy odor walks into your town and announces that your city will be destroyed by God in forty days. How would you repond? Why?

4. Are you surprised by the Ninevites' response to Jonah's proclamation (3:5-9)? Why or why not?

5. What does the Ninevites' response to Jonah's proclamation tell you about the people of Nineveh? (They seem to have been very aware of their wickedness. They seem to have believed that God was capable of destroying their city. They seem to have been very serious in their repentance.)

6. What does Jonah 3:10 tell us about God? (He is holy and just, demanding punishment for sin. However, He is also merciful and loving, willing to forgive those who repent of their wickedness.)

7. Why was Jonah so displeased and angry with God (4:1, 2)? (The Ninevites were enemies of Israel, so Jonah was probably looking forward to Nineveh's destruction. Perhaps he felt betrayed by God when the Lord showed compassion on Israel's enemy.)

8. What was God trying to teach Jonah with the vine-worm "object lesson" (4:5-10)? (Perhaps God was trying to show Jonah the folly of being more concerned about his personal discomfort than the souls of 120,000 people.)

9. The second time God asked Jonah if he had a right to be angry, Jonah responded, "I do" (4:9). Do you agree with Jonah? *Did* he have a right to be angry? Why or why not?

10. The Book of Jonah ends with the prophet still pouting about the dead vine and God's sparing of Nineveh. How do you think the story turned out? Do you think Jonah finally accepted God's reasoning? Or do you think the incidents in Nineveh created a rift between Jonah and God that was never mended? Explain your answer.

Point out that God is a giver of second chances. For instance, He gave Jonah a second chance to go to Nineveh as He'd instructed. He also gave the Ninevites a second chance to repent of their wickedness and save their city. Explain that God still gives people second chances, which is important because of our tendency to "mess up." Hand out copies of the reproducible sheet, "The God of Second Chances." Let kids work in pairs or small groups to come up with ways that they would explain God's second chances to each person on the sheet—and what a second chance might mean to each person. After a few minutes, ask volunteers to share what they came up with. Then give kids an opportunity to pray silently about an area of their life in which they need a second chance.

THE GOD OF
Second Chances

AMII

Amii, a high school junior, was part of an outreach group from her church. In the summer, the troupe would travel to churches in the area, performing skits and songs for youth group audiences. Part of the presentation involved each member of the troupe giving his or her personal testimony. Amii's testimony included her vow to keep herself sexually pure until marriage. Unfortunately, Amii failed to keep her vow. She became pregnant in late fall. Ashamed, Amii stopped attending church and hasn't spoken to anyone in her outreach group since she found out she was pregnant.

RUSSELL

Russell didn't have a very good reputation when he started attending youth group meetings. He'd been caught a couple of times trying to steal money out of lockers at school, and people were suspicious of him. But as the months went by, Russell seemed to change. Gradually he became part of the group and was accepted by the rest of the members. One day after a car wash fundraiser, the group treasurer asked Russell, who lived near the youth group leader, to drop off an envelope of money at the leader's house. Unfortunately, the temptation proved to be too much for Russell. He kept the money for himself and told everyone that it must have fallen out of his pocket on the way home. No one believed his story, but the church decided not to press charges against him. Russell hasn't been to a youth group meeting since the incident.

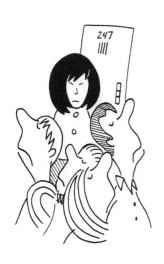

SONG LI

Song Li became jealous when she found out that Jennifer was dating her ex-boyfriend, so she started a rumor that Jennifer had contracted a sexually transmitted disease. Song Li was so convincing in her story that everyone believed her—including the boyfriend, who quickly dumped Jennifer. Jennifer was devastated by all of the jokes and rude comments that people whispered under their breath whenever she was around. But no matter how much she denied the rumor, no one believed her. Finally, in a tearful confrontation between Jennifer and Song Li in the middle of study hall, Song Li admitted that she'd made up the story. As a result, song Li quickly became an outcast at school. Angry at what she'd done to Jennifer, even Song Li's closest friends stopped hanging around with her.

MICAH

Good News, Bad News

God, through his prophet Micah, proclaims judgment on Israel. This message of doom is followed by a message of hope, establishing a roller coaster pattern for the entire book. Micah emphasizes both God's hatred of sin and His compassion for those who repent of their wickedness.

Have kids sit in a circle. You'll start the game by giving a "good news" statement (for example, **The good news is that John made it to today's meeting**). Someone else must then give a "bad news" twist to your statement (for example, "The bad news is that John's mind is on other things"). The next person must then give a "good news" twist to that statement, and so on. (A round might go like this: "The good news is that John got to drive his dad's car yesterday"; "The bad news is that he drove it into a tree"; "The good news is that the tree suffered very little damage"; "The bad news is that the car was totaled"; etc.) If a person fails to come up with an appropriate statement in five seconds, he or she is out. Continue until one person remains. Afterward, introduce the good news-bad news format of the Book of Micah.

DATE I USED THIS SESSION _____ GROUP I USED IT WITH _____

NOTES FOR NEXT TIME _____

_____

_____

1. **What's the most accurate prediction you've ever made?** (Some kids may have predicted that a certain sports team would win a championship. Others may have predicted that a certain guy and girl would start dating.) Point out that the Book of Micah contains several accurate predictions.

2. **If you had been one of the Israelites, how do you think you would have responded to Micah's announcement that "the Lord is coming from his dwelling place" (1:3)?** (We can assume that the Israelites were aware of their wicked condition, so it's likely that they weren't looking forward to a visit from the Lord.)

3. **What was the reason for God's prophecy against the Israelites (1:5)?** (God was punishing "the sins of the house of Israel"—which included idolatry [1:7].)

4. **Why do you think God chose to destroy Samaria, the capital of Israel, as part of His judgment against the people of Israel?** (The Israelites were a hard-hearted group of people. It took extreme measures—like destroying their capital city—to wake them up to their sinful condition.)

5. Read Micah 1:8, 9. **How do you think you would respond to a person like this who was prophesying against your nation? Why?**

6. **After identifying examples of Israel's corruption in Micah 2:1-11, God offers a message of hope in Micah 2:12, 13. What is God promising the Israelites here?** (God is promising that even though the Israelites will be punished and dispersed throughout the land, He will bring remnants of them back together someday and will serve as their leader.)

7. **The alternating messages of condemnation and hope continue throughout the book—Micah 3 is a condemnation; Micah 4–5 offers hope; Micah 6:1–7:7 is a condemnation; Micah 7:8-20 offers hope. What does this pattern tell you about God?** (As is demonstrated in almost all of the books of the minor prophets, God is just—He demands punishment for sin; however, He is also merciful and loving, forgiving those who repent.)

8. Based on the description in Micah 4, what do you think "the last days" (4:1) will be like? Explain.

9. Who is being referred to in Micah 5:2-5? Explain. (The passage is referring to Jesus, the Messiah and the Son of God, who was born in Bethlehem.)

10. While the Lord reads His "charges" against the Israelites concerning all of the wrong things they've done, He also gives a plain and simple reply as to what He requires of people who want to live for Him (6:8). What are these requirements? (To act justly, to love mercy, and to walk humbly with God.) Which of these requirements is most difficult for you? Why?

Remind group members again of the alternating themes of condemnation and hope throughout the Book of Micah. Suggest that, similarly, we face ups and downs in our lives today. Hand out copies of the reproducible sheet, "The Ultimate Roller Coaster." Give kids a few minutes to complete the sheet. When everyone is finished, ask volunteers to share some of the high points, low points, abrupt turns, etc., in their lives. Then read Isaiah 57:15. Affirm that God is always with us—in both the hills and valleys of our lives. Even when the valleys are the result of sin in our lives, God is willing to forgive us and restore our relationship with Him—if we sincerely repent of our sins.

THE ULTIMATE
Roller Coaster

You've probably heard the saying, "Life is full of ups and downs." Well, we're asking you to be a little more specific. Think of your life (or at least the past couple of years) as a roller coaster. What kinds of "hills" (high points) and "valleys" (low points) have you experienced? What's the most "up" you've ever been? What's been the lowest experience of your life? What situations have thrown you for a loop? Which ones have caused you to do 180° turns in the way you think or the things you do? Label the sections of the roller coaster ride below to represent various events and situations in your life.

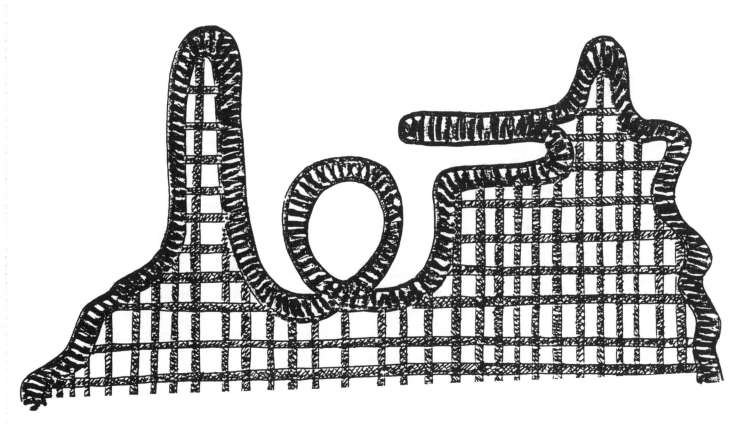

NAHUM

Nineveh: The Next Generation

After repenting of their wickedness and being spared by God during the days of Jonah, the Ninevites revert to their evil ways. God sends another prophet, Nahum, to pronounce judgment on Nineveh. After testifying to God's kindness and sternness, Nahum witnesses the destruction of Nineveh—a destruction that brings joy to the people of Judah.

Have kids form teams. Give the teams five minutes to list as many movie sequels as they can think of. When time is up, have each team read its list aloud. If a team reads a title that appears on another team's list, that title must be crossed off both (or all) lists. The team with the most remaining titles is the winner. [A more active option is to have teams create movie trailers (one- to two-minute "previews" to be shown in theaters) for the most unusual sequels they can think of. (How about *The Sound of Music II: Back into Austria*?) Encourage kids to have fun with this. After a few minutes, have each team perform its trailer for the rest of the group.] Use the idea of a sequel to introduce the Book of Nahum, which might be considered a sequel to the Book of Jonah.

DATE I USED THIS SESSION _____ GROUP I USED IT WITH _____

NOTES FOR NEXT TIME _____

_____

_____

1. Have you ever had someone try to take advantage of you after you did something nice for him or her? Without naming names, what were the circumstances? What happened? How did you feel?

2. Read Jonah 3. **When we last left Nineveh in the Bible, what was going on?** (The Lord sent Jonah to Nineveh to warn the Ninevites that God was going to destroy their city. The Ninevites immediately repented of their wickedness and begged God to relent. The Lord showed compassion on the city and spared it—much to Jonah's chagrin.)

3. **Nahum 1:2 says that the Lord is a jealous and avenging God; the next verse says that the Lord is slow to anger. Do these two descriptions fit together? If so, how?** (The Lord acts justly in judging His enemies, but He also gives people an opportunity to repent of their wickedness.)

4. Read Nahum 1:7. **When has God been "a refuge in times of trouble" for you? What were the circumstances? How did God serve as a refuge?**

5. **What can we assume from the Lord's proclamation in Nahum 1:8-14?** (The Ninevites had reverted back to their evil ways and had done wickedness in the sight of the Lord. As a result, the Lord was now going to bring judgment on the city of Nineveh.)

6. **Why would the destruction of Nineveh have been "good news" for the people of Judah** (1:15)**?** (Not only were the Ninevites longtime enemies of the people of Judah, they were also noted for their extreme brutality and oppression. The fall of Nineveh was something the Judahites had been looking forward to for quite a while.)

7. **How do you think the Ninevites responded to this second judgment against them? After all, they'd been spared when Jonah prophesied against them. Do you think they believed they might be spared again? Explain.**

8. **How do you think Nahum's words in Nahum 2:2 might have made the Ninevites feel? Why?** (It must have been like "rubbing salt in the wound" to know that while Nineveh was going to be destroyed, Israel was going to prosper.)

9. How, if at all, has the story of Nineveh affected the way you think about obeying God and living a righteous life? Explain.

10. Some people try to take advantage of God's mercy, doing the things *they* want to do, banking on the fact that God will always be there to give them a fresh start when they repent. What's wrong with this type of thinking? (People who are truly repentant give their best effort to live a God-pleasing life instead of just using God as a "safety valve.")

Hand out copies of the reproducible sheet, "Taking God Lightly." Let kids work in pairs or small groups to complete the sheet. After a few minutes, have group members share their responses. Ask volunteers to share which attributes and characteristics of God they're most likely to take lightly. Then, as a group, brainstorm a list of strategies for keeping God's attributes and characteristics in perspective. Close the session in prayer, praising God for His specific attributes and characteristics.

Taking God Lightly

When Jonah prophesied that the city of Nineveh would be destroyed, the Ninevites "cleaned up their act" and repented of their wickedness. As a result, God forgave them and spared their city. Shortly thereafter, however, the Ninevites returned to their wicked ways—so God destroyed their city. The Ninevites took God's forgiveness lightly—and they suffered the consequences. Below we've listed several of God's attributes and characteristics. For each one, write down a specific example of how someone today might take that attribute/characteristic lightly—and what the consequences might be.

GOD'S WISDOM
Example: A person becomes aware of God's plan for his life, yet chooses to pursue his own agenda.
Consequences: The person misses out on some great opportunities for his future.

GOD'S LOVE
Example:

Consequences:

GOD'S HOLINESS
Example:

Consequences:

GOD'S MERCY
Example:

Consequences:

GOD'S IMMUTABILITY
(His unchanging nature)
Example:

Consequences:

GOD'S OMNIPRESENCE
(His ability to be everywhere at once)
Example:

Consequences:

GOD'S OMNISCIENCE
(His awareness of everything)
Example:

Consequences:

GOD'S OMNIPOTENCE
(His complete power over everything)
Example:

Consequences:

HABAKKUK

The "Whys" Guy

The Book of Habakkuk is written as a dialogue between Habakkuk and God. First, Habakkuk questions God about why the evil in Judah isn't purged. God informs Habakkuk that Babylon will do the purging. Habakkuk then asks why God would use a nation more wicked than Israel to punish Israel. God responds that Babylon also will be punished and that those who remain in God will receive blessing. Habakkuk concludes the book by reaffirming his trust in God.

(Needed: List of questions, prizes)

Before the session, compile a list of intriguing questions. The list might include questions like "Where does chalk go when it's erased?" "Why is it important to keep a little lint in your pocket?" and "What did people do before gravity was invented?" To begin the session, have kids form pairs. Read one of the questions from your list; then give each pair one minute to come up with an answer. Award a point to the team that comes up with the most plausible (or funniest) response. Continue with the rest of the questions on your list. At the end of the activity, award prizes to the pair with the most points. Afterward, explain that the prophet Habakkuk asked God several tough questions—and got some interesting answers.

DATE I USED THIS SESSION _____ GROUP I USED IT WITH _____

NOTES FOR NEXT TIME _____

_____

_____

1. What's the most difficult question you've ever been asked? How did you answer it? What's the most difficult question you've ever asked someone else? What answer did you get?

2. The Book of Habakkuk is written as a dialogue between Habakkuk and God. In the first part of the book, Habakkuk asks God a couple of questions. What's Habakkuk's first question (1:2-4)? (Habakkuk asks why the Lord tolerates injustice and wickedness among the people of Judah.) Have you ever asked God a similar question? If so, when?

3. What do you suppose prompted Habakkuk to ask this question? (Perhaps as one of the faithful, godly people in Judah, Habakkuk was tired of seeing evil people prosper and flaunt their wickedness without being punished for it.)

4. How do you think God feels about being questioned? (It depends on the spirit of the questioner. If a person is truly trying to understand God's ways, God will honor his or her question. If a person is trying to second-guess or cast doubts on God's wisdom, God probably will not honor the person's question.)

5. What is Habakkuk's attitude as he questions God? (Although he seems to be complaining, it appears as though Habakkuk is truly trying to understand God's ways.)

6. How does God answer Habakkuk's first question (1:5-11)? (God tells Habakkuk that He is going to raise up the Babylonians, a "ruthless and impetuous people," to bring judgment on the people of Judah.)

7. God's response sparks another question from Habakkuk. What is it (1:12–2:1)? (Habakkuk asks why the Lord would use the Babylonians—who were much more wicked than the people of Judah—to execute judgment on the people of Judah.)

8. **How does God answer Habakkuk's second question** (2:2-19)**?** (The Lord makes it clear that Babylon will also be judged. The corrupt destroyer will itself be destroyed.)

9. **Which of the deeds of the Lord mentioned in Habakkuk 3:2-15 is most impressive to you? Why?**

10. **What is Habakkuk saying in the final part of his prayer** (3:16-19)**?** (Even though Habakkuk may not understand the Lord's timing for or methods of judgment, he will trust God and wait patiently for Him.)

(Needed: Chalkboard and chalk or newsprint and marker)

Hand out copies of the reproducible sheet, "If You Could Ask God . . ." When the five minutes are up, ask group members to share some of their questions. Write on the board any questions that are mentioned by more than one person. Then, as a group, come up with strategies for answering some of these questions. Certainly many answers can be found in the Bible. Others can be found in prayer. Still others (like questions concerning God's will for a person's life) may be revealed gradually over time. Close the session by reading I Corinthians 13:12 and Hebrews 11:1. Assure group members that *all* of our questions will be answered eventually. Encourage kids not to allow unanswered questions to affect their relationship with God.

If You Could Ask God...

There's a phone call for you—it's from God. He's heard that you've got some questions for Him, and He's ready to answer them. This is your golden opportunity to ask Him about anything you don't understand. But you can leave Him "on hold" on the phone for only five minutes. So take the next five minutes to come up with a list of questions you'd like to ask. We've provided some categories to get you started.

Friends
God's will for your life
Sex
Family
Finding a marriage partner
Crime
Hunger and poverty
Disease and sickness

ZEPHANIAH

The Day of the Lord

Zephaniah, like some of the other minor prophets, prophesies of the coming "day of the Lord." Zephaniah emphasizes that Judah will be judged at this time and punished along with other nations. This prophecy contradicts the people of Judah's belief that they're exempt from God's wrath. And, like some of the other minor prophets, Zephaniah follows up his message of doom by proclaiming God's mercy and predicting the eventual restoration of Judah.

Have group members form a circle. Explain that you will call out a category— colors, fruits, major league baseball teams, etc. One at a time (proceeding around the circle), group members must name items in that category. (For instance, if the category is major league baseball teams, kids might name the Chicago Cubs, New York Yankees, St. Louis Cardinals, etc.) If a person repeats an item that's already been named or if a person can't think of an item in that category in five seconds, he or she is out. Continue the game until only one person remains. Use the idea of repetition to introduce the Book of Zephaniah, which repeats a theme found in previous books of the minor prophets: the "day of the Lord."

DATE I USED THIS SESSION _____ GROUP I USED IT WITH _____

NOTES FOR NEXT TIME _____

_____

_____

1. If the Lord were to punish our society today for its wickedness, how do you think He might do it? Why?

2. How would you describe the Lord's tone or attitude in **Zephaniah 1:2, 3?** (He seems to be completely fed up with the people's wickedness.)

3. Zephaniah certainly wasn't the first prophet to warn Judah about God's impending judgment of all nations. How do you think the people of Judah responded to his message? Why?

4. Why do you suppose the people of Judah required so many warnings of God's judgment? (They seem to have been under the impression that since they were God's chosen people, they would be spared God's wrath.)

5. How can you convince people to believe something that they don't want to believe? Compare group members' responses with Zephaniah's graphic description of God's judgment of Judah in Zephaniah 1:4–2:3.

6. Hand out copies of the reproducible sheet, "Mapping Out the Day of the Lord." As you go through the descriptions of God's judgments on various nations in the Book of Zephaniah, have group members draw pictures in each country to represent the destruction going on there. For instance, kids might draw storm clouds over Judah (1:15). **What can we learn about the people of Judah from God's pronouncement of judgment on them** (1:4–2:3)**?** (They seem to have been heavily involved in idol worship. The wickedness was widespread—people of all different walks of life are singled out for judgment.)

7. What does it mean to "seek the Lord" (2:3)? (Seeking the Lord involves repenting of wickedness and following His ways.) **What kinds of things keep people from seeking the Lord today? Explain.**

8. Moab and Ammon were going to be destroyed because of their pride (2:10). **Why is pride so potentially harmful?**

How can you prevent pride from causing problems in your life?

9. **How do you explain the sudden change of tone in Zephaniah 3:14-20?** (Zephaniah ends the book on a positive note—perhaps as an encouragement to the faithful remnant in Judah—by affirming that God will restore Israel after His judgment is completed.)

10. **Do you think people today are judged as harshly for their sins as the people in Zephaniah's time were? Explain.** (God's attitude toward wickedness hasn't changed. He still demands punishment for sin. However, because Christ has already taken the punishment for our sins, we have the opportunity for a renewed relationship with God. Those who refuse to accept Christ's gift of salvation will receive full punishment for their sins.)

(Needed: Bible reference resources)

After you finish the "Q & A" section, ask volunteers to display their completed maps and explain what the various pictures represent. Acknowledge that the Book of Zephaniah—along with several other books of the minor prophets—paints a fairly intimidating portrait of God. To help group members get a more balanced view of God, go to His Word. Have kids form teams. Give each team a Bible concordance or some other reference resource. Instruct the teams to locate words like "love," "mercy," "comfort," "grace," "forgiveness," etc., and then look up Bible passages in which those words are used in relation to God. (If you're short on time, you might assign one or two words to each team.) After a few minutes, have each team read one or two of its passages. As you wrap up the session, encourage kids to choose one or two of the passages to memorize. Emphasize the importance of maintaining a balanced view of God—one that includes both His holiness and His love.

Mapping Out the Day of the Lord

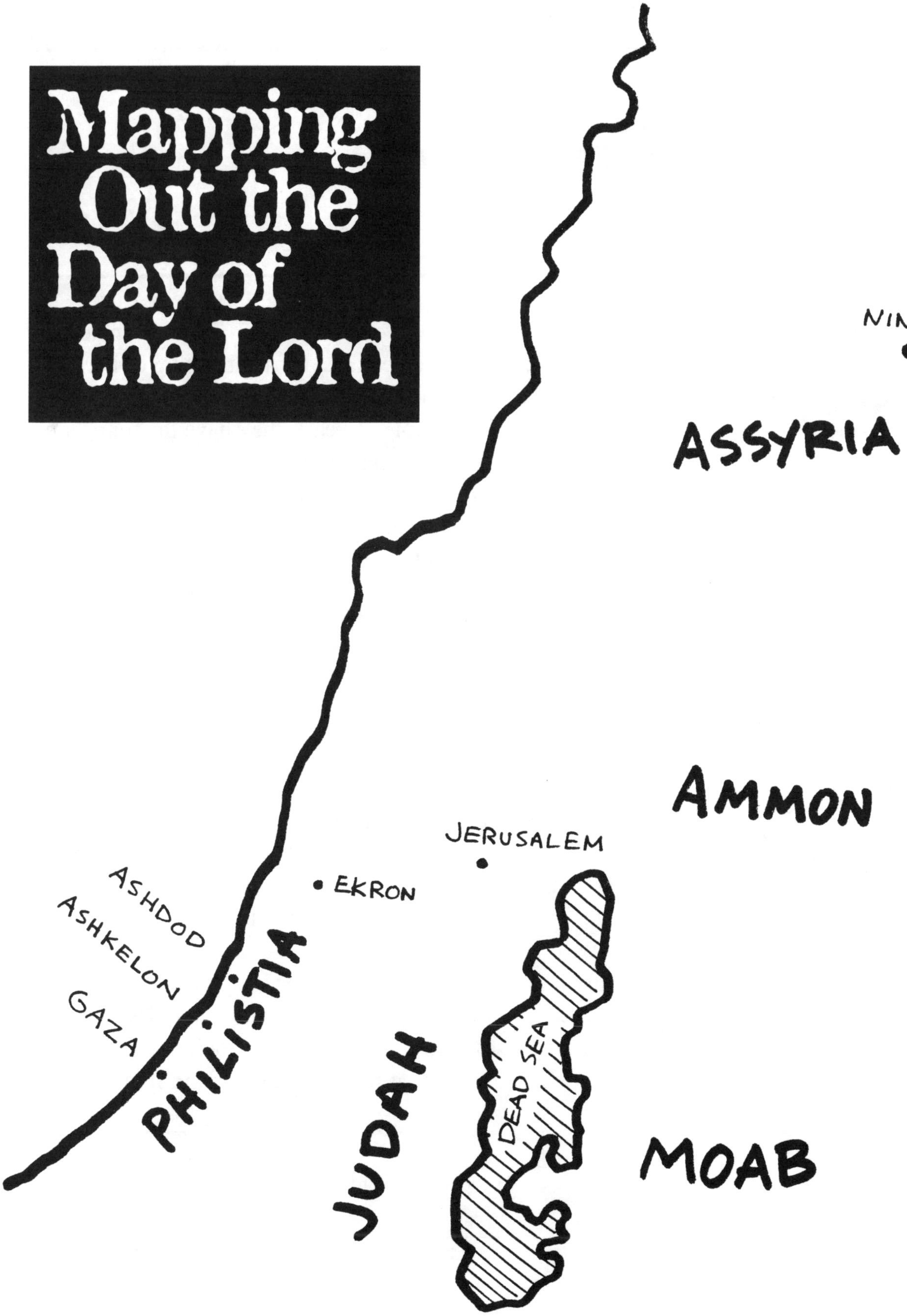

NINEVEH

ASSYRIA

AMMON

JERUSALEM

ASHDOD

ASHKELON

EKRON

GAZA

PHILISTIA

JUDAH

DEAD SEA

MOAB

HAGGAI

Priorities

More than fifty years have passed since Jerusalem was destroyed and the Israelites were exiled from Judah. Babylon has been defeated by the Persians. Cyrus, the king of Persia, allows the exiled Israelites to return to Jerusalem to rebuild the temple. Within a couple of years, they have the foundation of the temple rebuilt. But pressure from opposing nations temporarily halts their efforts. When Darius becomes king of Persia, he allows the Israelites to resume the reconstruction. But the Israelites begin making excuses for postponing the rebuilding efforts—so God sends Haggai to speak to the Israelites about putting their own priorities ahead of God's.

(Needed: Legos or Tinkertoys, pictures, prizes)

Before the session, build a structure using Legos or Tinkertoys. Take several pictures of the structure. To begin the session, have kids form two teams. Give each team a set of Legos or Tinkertoys. Display the pictures. Explain that the teams will be competing to see which one can re-create the structure in the pictures first. Emphasize that the re-creation must be *exact*. Award prizes to the winning team. Use the idea of rebuilding a structure to introduce the Book of Haggai, in which the Israelites start to rebuild the temple in Jerusalem.

DATE I USED THIS SESSION _____ GROUP I USED IT WITH _____

NOTES FOR NEXT TIME _____

_____

_____

1. What's the most ambitious project you [...] led? Did you complete it? If so, how long did it take? [...] did you feel when you completed it?

2. What kinds of things might cause someone to lose interest in or quit working on an especially ambitious project? Explain.

3. The events in the Book of Haggai take place more than fifty years after Jerusalem was destroyed and the Israelites were exiled from Judah. How might that fact explain the people's attitude in Haggai 1:2? (The Israelites had been in exile for so long that many of them had no memories of the original temple in Jerusalem. As a result, they felt no burning need to rebuild it.)

4. What does God's response in Haggai 1:4 tell you about the priorities of the Israelites? (They were more concerned about their own needs than about the things of God.)

5. The Israelites were more concerned about their own houses than about the Lord's temple (1:4). What are some things today that might be given a higher priority than the things of God?

6. What is God saying in Haggai 1:5-11? (Because the Israelites' focus was on their own lives, on their material possessions, the Lord withheld blessing from them—by sending famine, drought, etc.—so that they wouldn't have enough. But rather than turning to God to get their satisfaction, the Israelites just complained that they didn't have enough.)

7. Haggai's words from the Lord shook the Israelites out of their lethargic, "me-first" mind-set and got them working on finishing the rebuilding of the temple (1:13-15). What do you think it might take to shake someone today out of a lethargic, "me-first" attitude? Explain.

8. If you'd been one of the workers who was rebuilding the temple, how do you think God's words in Haggai 2:1-9 might have affected you? Why?

9. What point was God—through Haggai—making with the "consecrated meat" analogy (2:10-19)? (He was warning the Israelites that even though they were back in the holy land, that holiness didn't make them pure. The people were still required to obey the Lord.)

10. If you had to sum up the message of the Book of Haggai in one sentence, what would it be? How might that message apply to the lives of people today? Explain.

Hand out copies of the reproducible sheet, "The Project." Give group members a few minutes to complete the sheet. When everyone is finished, ask volunteers to share the details of their projects. Emphasize to your group members the importance of encouraging and helping one another with these tasks. At future meetings, have group members report on the progress of their work. Close the session in prayer, asking God to bless the work of your group members as they attempt to complete their tasks.

THE PROJECT

Rebuilding the temple of Jerusalem was an enormous task that required a lot of hard work. The Israelites faced several obstacles during the project. But they had a goal in mind—an end result that they wanted to see. They were motivated by the fact that what they were doing pleased God. And because they were doing God's will, He blessed their efforts.

How about you? What significant, God-pleasing task might you begin? Perhaps you might consider setting up an ambitious personal Bible study schedule with the goal of reading through the entire Bible in a year. Or you might consider starting a small-group Bible study. Or you might consider trying to raise a certain amount of money to donate to a missions organization.

Write the task you choose on the sign below. Then, on the individual bricks, write down the things you'll need to do in order to complete your task. Be as specific and detailed as possible. (For instance, if you want to start a small-group Bible study, you'll need to choose who will be in the small group, decide what study material to use, plan when and where to meet, etc.) Outside the building, write down various kinds of opposition that you might face as you work on your project. (Opposition might include things like boredom, apathy, scheduling problems, busyness, etc.) Above the building, write down some specific ways God might bless your efforts. (For instance, He might send friends to help and encourage you.)

ZECHARIAH

Night Visions

OVERVIEW

Like Haggai, Zechariah rebukes the Israelites in order to motivate them to finish rebuilding the temple in Jerusalem. Zechariah has a series of night visions concerning the Israelites' return to God and God's return to them. Zechariah ends his book with prophecies concerning the coming Messiah and His kingdom.

OPENING ACT

Begin the session with some impromptu roleplays. Ask four volunteers to come to the front of the room. Choose one of them to be the narrator. Instruct this person to describe the weirdest dream he or she can think of. The dream should involve three characters—who will be portrayed by the other three volunteers. Everything the narrator describes should be performed by the other actors. For instance, if the narrator says, "Suddenly I saw a frog hopping in slow motion," one of the volunteers must start hopping in slow motion. Encourage the narrator to have fun with his or her descriptions (within the boundaries of good taste). After a few minutes, give your performers a round of applause. Continue the activity with other volunteers as time allows. Afterward, use the topic of dreams to introduce the Book of Zechariah, in which Zechariah has a series of night visions.

DATE I USED THIS SESSION _____ GROUP I USED IT WITH _____

NOTES FOR NEXT TIME_____

_____

_____

1. How often do you dream? In general, what kinds of things do you dream about? Why do you suppose that is?

2. Can you "interpret" your dreams? In other words, do you know *why* you dream about the things you do? Explain.

3. Read Zechariah 1:3. **Why do you think the Lord required that the Israelites return to Him before He returned to them?** (It was the Israelites' sin that messed up the relationship in the first place. The Israelites were responsible to make the first move in restoring the relationship by repenting.)

4. Hand out copies of the reproducible sheet, "Vision Quest." Give group members a few minutes to read the passages and complete the exercise. When everyone is finished, go through the answers as a group. (The correct responses are as follows: [1] c; [2] d; [3] e; [4] a; [5] f; [6] b; [7] h; [8] g.) Refer to the sheet periodically during your discussion of Zechariah's visions. **Why do you think God used visions to communicate with Zechariah? Explain.**

5. **What common theme do you find in each of Zechariah's visions?** (God offers encouragement and comfort for the Israelites, promising them that a great future awaits them.)

6. **If you'd been one of the Israelites, which vision do you think would have been most significant to you? Why?**

7. **What is the Lord accusing the Israelites of in Zechariah 7:4-7?** (Being insincere and selfish in their fasting.) **Do you think it's possible for people to be insincere and selfish in their worship practices today? Explain.** (People who worship in order to impress others with their "spirituality" and people who worship in order to receive some kind of reward from the Lord are being insincere and selfish.)

8. **How might a person today obey the four commands of the Lord in Zechariah 7:9, 10? Give specific examples.**

9. Read Zechariah 14:1-21. **Describe what you think this period of time will be like.**

10. **How might a non-Christian react to the "day of the Lord" description in Zechariah 14? Why? How would you explain the passage to a non-Christian friend?**

Wrap up the session with a celebration of the fact that the ultimate future of the world is set—God will emerge victorious. Read Zechariah 14:9. Then have group members list things that will be different about the world when God is "king over the whole earth." Close the session in prayer, thanking God for the assurance we can have regarding our future.

Vision Quest

Match each of Zechariah's visions with the interpretation that sounds most plausible to you.

1. A man among myrtle trees (1:7-17)

a. God would send His servant, Jesus, to remove the sin of the people.

2. Four horns and four craftsmen (1:18-21)

b. A curse was being sent out to thieves and lawbreakers in the land.

3. A man with a measuring line (2:1-13)

c. God's messengers would go in all directions to deal with the nations of the earth.

4. Clean garments for the high priest (3:1-10)

d. The temple would be rebuilt and the Israelites would prosper again.

5. The gold lampstand and the two olive trees (4:1-14)

e. Jerusalem would again be populated. The nations who had persecuted Israel would be punished.

6. The flying scroll (5:1-4)

f. Zerubbabel would complete the temple, which would be attended to by two people.

7. The woman in a basket (5:5-11)

g. Judah's enemies would be terrified and defeated.

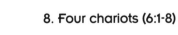

8. Four chariots (6:1-8)

h. Israel's wickedness would be removed from Judah, but allowed to flourish in Babylon.

MALACHI

A Final Warning

About seventy years after the temple was rebuilt, Nehemiah returned to Jerusalem to oversee the rebuilding of the walls around Jerusalem. When the project was completed, Nehemiah went back to serve King Artaxerxes in Persia. In Nehemiah's absence, the Israelites fall into sin once again. The Lord sends His prophet Malachi to condemn the sins of the people and to warn them about the "day of the Lord."

(Needed: Book of historical dates, index cards, tape)

Before the session, find a book that lists the dates of several historical events—the writing of the King James Bible, the discovery of electricity, the signing of the Declaration of Independence, the first baseball game, and so forth. (You might also want to include other less historical dates like the birth dates of your pastor and some of your kids.) Write each event—but not the date—on a separate index card. Have kids form two teams. Tape one of the index cards on each group member. Explain that the first team to arrange its members according to the chronological order of their assigned events is the winner. Afterward, point out that not only is Malachi's book the last one in the Old Testament, but that Malachi is also most likely the last prophet in the Old Testament era.

DATE I USED THIS SESSION _____ GROUP I USED IT WITH _____

NOTES FOR NEXT TIME _____

_____

_____

1. Do you act any differently when your parents or some other authority figures are around than you do when you're alone or with your friends? If so, how do you act differently? Why?

2. Nehemiah had come from Persia to help the Israelites rebuild the wall in Jerusalem. While he was in Jerusalem, the Israelites were faithful to the Lord. But when Nehemiah left to return to Persia, the Israelites fell into sin again. What does this tell you about the Israelites? **Explain.** (They were undependable. They were spiritually immature. They seemed to be lost without a leader.)

3. What kind of honor and respect is "due" God (1:6)? What are some ways to show honor and respect to God?

4. In Malachi 1:6, the Israelites ask God, "How have we shown contempt for your name?" How does God answer that question (1:7-14)? (He tells the Israelites that they have been offering defiled food to Him on their altars—a clear violation of His law.)

5. How do people show contempt for God's name today? **Explain.**

6. How had the performance of the priests changed since the time of Levi, the man from whom all of Israel's priests had descended (2:1-9)? (The priests of Malachi's time did not have their hearts set on honoring God. As a result, they led people astray with their false wisdom.)

7. What does the example of the priests tell you about the responsibilities of a Christian leader? (The first and foremost goal of all Christian leaders should be to honor God. Many lives can be negatively affected if a Christian leader fails to honor God in his or her actions.)

8. Malachi compares the Lord's judgment to a refiner's fire, which was used to purify things like gold and silver (3:2-4). What are some areas of a Christian's life today that might be purified in God's "refinery"?

9. God accuses the Israelites of robbing Him by not bringing "the whole tithe into the storehouse" (3:6-12). What's the big deal about tithing? After all, it's not like God needs our money. (Tithing is a way of acknowledging that everything we receive comes from God. It also shows our willingness to give back to Him a portion of what He's given to us.)

10. Of course, we couldn't get through a study of one of the books of the minor prophets without mentioning the "day of the Lord" (4:1-6). How can the Israelites escape God's judgment? (Repent of their wickedness; "revere" God's name; "remember" God's law.)

Point out that the Old Testament prophets were accurate in their predictions regarding the coming of Jesus—His birthplace, His suffering, His death, etc. These prophets also predicted a glorious (we know it as a *second*) coming of Jesus. Briefly discuss what this as-yet-unfulfilled prophecy means to your group members. Then point out that just as the Lord was faithful in fulfilling His prophecies, He's also faithful to keep promises like those found in Psalm 32:8; Psalm 138:7; and John 14:2, 3. Hand out copies of the reproducible sheet, "The Big Difference." Instruct group members to fill out the first column according to how they might respond to each situation if they weren't expecting God's help; instruct them to fill out the second column according to how they might respond if they're expecting God's help. After a few minutes, ask volunteers to share their responses. Close the session in prayer, thanking God for His faithfulness in fulfilling His prophecies and keeping His promises.

THE **BIG** DIFFERENCE

NEED
SOME
HELP
?

In the first column, write down how you might respond to each situation if you weren't expecting God's help. In the second column, write down how you might respond if you're expecting God's help.

	Not Expecting God's Help	**Expecting God's Help**
A close friend or family member dies.		
A friend confides to you that he or she is considering suicide.		
Your parents tell you that there's no way they can afford to send you to college.		
You have an accident that leaves you blind.		
You overhear your parents talking about getting a divorce.		
You're being pressured to declare a "gang allegiance" in your neighborhood.		
Everyone at school makes fun of you because you have some kind of physical defect.		
You feel friendless and lonely.		
The person you're dating is pressuring you to have sex.		